TE

Visit our How To website at www.howto.co.uk

At **www.howto.co.uk** you can engage in conversation with our authors – all of whom have 'been there and done that' in their specialist fields. You can get access to special offers and additional content but most importantly you will be able to engage with, and become a part of, a wide and growing community of people just like yourself.

At **www.howto.co.uk** you'll be able to talk and share tips with people who have similar interests and are facing similar challenges in their lives. People who, just like you, have the desire to change their lives for the better – be it through moving to a new country, starting a new business, growing their own vegetables, or writing a novel.

At **www.howto.co.uk** you'll find the support and encouragement you need to help make your aspirations a reality.

You can go direct to **www.do-your-own-divorce.co.uk** which is part of the main How To site.

How To Books strives to present authentic, inspiring, practical information in their books. Now, when you buy a title from **How To Books**, you get even more than just words on a page.

DO YOUR OWN DIVORCE

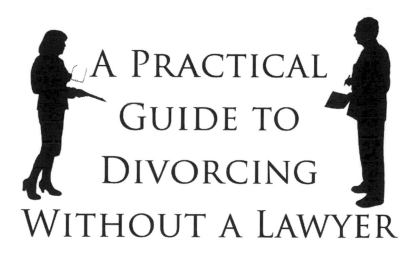

A PRACTICAL GUIDE TO DIVORCING WITHOUT A LAWYER

JOHN BOLCH

howtobooks

For my son James

Published by How To Books Ltd
Spring Hill House, Spring Hill Road
Begbroke, Oxford OX5 1RX
Tel: (01865) 375794. Fax: (01865) 379162
info@howtobooks.co.uk
www.howtobooks.co.uk

How To Books greatly reduce the carbon footprint of their books by
sourcing their typesetting and printing in the UK.

British Library Cataloguing in Publication Data
A catalogue record for this book is available from the British Library

ISBN: 978 1 84528 355 1

Produced for How To Books by Deer Park Productions, Tavistock
Typeset by Kestrel Data, Exeter
Printed and bound by Cromwell Press Group, Trowbridge, Wiltshire

Contents

Introduction

WHO THIS BOOK IS FOR

Anyone who is not a family lawyer! That is, anyone who is seeking or contemplating a divorce, or anyone whose spouse has issued divorce proceedings against them. Even if you are separating from your spouse and do not wish to divorce at this time, this book will be useful to you as many of the principles remain the same, especially with regard to arrangements for children and sorting out finances (see also the section on separation agreements below).

WHY DO YOUR OWN DIVORCE?

To save money! Even if the divorce is completely straightforward, and there are no arrangements for children and finances to sort out, a solicitor will typically charge between £500 and £1000 to deal with the divorce for you, not including court fees. If there are arrangements for children or finances to sort out, then the solicitor's fees are likely to be many times that sum. Even if you cannot deal with everything yourself, dealing with one aspect (say, the divorce itself) without a solicitor will result in you making considerable savings in legal costs.

WHAT IF MY SPOUSE HAS A SOLICITOR?

Don't worry, this does not have to mean that you are at a disadvantage. This book will take you through all of the procedures and deal with all of the principles that you need to know to ensure that you achieve a similar result, in a similar time, to what you would achieve if you had a solicitor yourself. Your spouse's solicitor will have to deal with you in the same way they would deal with your solicitor.

If possible, keep all communication with your spouse's solicitor civil (and they should do likewise). Do not use letters as an opportunity to say all the bad things you want to say about your spouse – this will get you nowhere and reduce the chance of reaching agreement. Keep everything relevant to the issues at hand, as indicated by this book.

Keep copies of all correspondence with your spouse's solicitor and make a dated note of any telephone conversations.

WHAT IF I NEED A SOLICITOR MYSELF?

I believe that, with the help of this book, the majority of readers will be able to deal with their divorce and sort out arrangements for children and finances without having to instruct a solicitor. However, there may be times when matters become too complex for any reasonably capable person to deal with without legal help, and some occasions when you will have to instruct a solicitor, for example when a house sale or transfer is required (mortgage lenders will insist that a solicitor or licensed conveyancer deal with such transactions). This book will always inform you when this is the case and, where appropriate, give you some indication of the likely cost involved.

If you do need to instruct a solicitor (other than simply for conveyancing work) then I would recommend that you consult one who is a member of Resolution, an organisation of family lawyers whose members follow a code of practice that promotes a non-confrontational approach to family problems. Such an approach reduces animosity, increases the chance of settlement (thereby reducing costs) and, above all, is in the best interests of children. For details of Resolution, including how to find a Resolution member, see Appendix 2.

Do I WANT A DIVORCE?

This may sound like a stupid question – if you're reading this book, you've already decided that you want a divorce. However, before rushing to court you should ask yourself: am I absolutely certain that my marriage has irretrievably broken down? Remember, if it has not then the action of issuing divorce proceedings is likely to put an end to any chance of a reconciliation. If you are in any doubt, consider seeking marriage guidance at Relate (for details, see Appendix 2). If your spouse does not want to go to Relate, they can always advise you on your own. If it is clear that you and your spouse will separate (or if you have already separated), but it is not clear that the marriage is over, consider entering into a separation agreement, as described in the next section.

SEPARATION AGREEMENTS

It is quite common that a husband and wife will separate but neither will want to take divorce proceedings at that time. They will, however, want to sort out financial arrangements, and ensure that those arrangements are finalised (so far as possible – arrangements can only be completely finalised by a court order when a divorce takes place). In these circumstances, a written separation agreement (or deed) is usually drawn up. A typical example separation agreement can be found in Appendix 1. Note that such an agreement cannot deal with pension sharing (see Chapter 4), which requires a court order.

Note also that, as indicated above, separation agreements are not 100% final, as they do not prevent the court in any future divorce proceedings from ordering a different financial settlement, on the application of either party. However, courts do like parties to agree matters and therefore if the settlement set out in the separation agreement is broadly reasonable then the court is less likely to order something different. The principles set out in Chapter 4 will help you to reach an agreement that is broadly reasonable. If the parties have both taken some legal advice before signing the agreement (or even if one party has and the other party has chosen not to) then the court is even more likely to uphold it.

Two other points on separation agreements: firstly, they often include a term along the lines that if the parties are still separated after two years have elapsed since the date of the separation, then either party may then issue divorce proceedings on the basis of two year's separation, and the other party will consent to the divorce (see Chapter 1, and paragraph 9 of the example separation agreement). Note, however, that such consent is not binding – consent has to be given to the court at the time of the divorce proceedings, and either party may change their mind before the proceedings are issued. However, a clause such as the one in the example agreement is all that can be done at the time of the separation, and is obviously an indication that both parties intend to consent. The second point is that the clause does not preclude either party from issuing divorce proceedings before the two year period has elapsed, for example if the other party commits adultery during that period.

What if the terms of a separation agreement are breached, for example one party refuses to implement the agreed terms of a financial/property settlement? Well, a separation agreement is a contract, so I suppose that theoretically the other party could sue for breach of contract, but I've never heard of it being done. In practice, that party would issue divorce proceedings and apply to the divorce court for a financial/property settlement – see Chapter 4. If a child maintenance agreement is breached, that party can make an application for child support to the Child Support Agency – see Chapter 3.

LIMITATIONS OF THIS BOOK

A book this size could not possibly cover every eventuality, and nor does it attempt to. For example, the book will not deal in detail with defended divorces, complex financial issues or children disputes, or serious cases of domestic violence. I will try to deal with the most common situations, but even something that starts off quite straightforward can become complex or out of the ordinary. In such cases, I will try to give basic advice and, where possible, an indication of where to go for further help.

HOW TO USE THIS BOOK

Read the relevant parts of this book before taking any action. So, if you want a divorce, have no minor children and have no finances to sort out, read Chapter 1, the consent order sections of Chapter 4 and Chapter 7. If you want a divorce, have minor children and finances to sort out, you will need to read Chapters 1 to 4, Chapters 6 and 7.

A large part of this book comprises advice on how to prepare the various documents required to comply with the relevant procedure (divorce, children application, financial application, and so on). In most cases the advice refers to example documents contained in Appendix 1. I suggest that you read through the example document before reading the advice upon how to complete it, which is contained in the main text.

Note that in this book the law is as stated at May 2009, as are all fees quoted in the book.

ABOUT THE AUTHOR

I qualified as a solicitor in 1985. Since then I have specialised in divorce and family matters. I was one of the first members of the Law Society's Family Law Panel (now the Family Law Accreditation Scheme) and am a long-time member of Resolution, formerly the Solicitors Family Law Association. I am also the author of the Family Lore blog (www.familylore.co.uk) and Family Lore *Focus* (www.familylorefocus.com).

ACKNOWLEDGEMENTS

Thanks to Sharon and Bev for encouraging me to get this book completed, Inga Rolfe for help with the typing, Yvonne Stevenson for encouragement and proof reading and Mike Semple Piggot for his help and encouragement. Any errors in the book are, of course, solely my responsibility.

1

Divorce

A BRIEF OUTLINE OF DIVORCE PROCEDURE

The procedure on an undefended divorce is essentially a five-stage process:

1   The party taking the divorce proceedings (the 'petitioner') issues (i.e. files with the court) the divorce petition together with supporting documents. The court will process the papers and send copies to the other party, along with an acknowledgement of service form.

2   The other party (the 'respondent') completes and files the acknowledgement of service, indicating (amongst other things) whether or not he or she intends to defend the divorce. The court will send a copy of the form to the petitioner.

3   If the divorce is not defended, the petitioner can then apply to the court for the divorce to proceed. This is known as 'applying for directions'.

4   If the court is satisfied that the petitioner is entitled to a divorce, it will fix a date for the pronouncement of the decree nisi, and notify both parties. It is not normally necessary to attend court when the decree nisi is pronounced.

5   After six weeks have elapsed since the date the decree nisi is pronounced the petitioner can apply for the decree absolute, finalising the divorce. The court will then seal the decree absolute and send copies to both parties.

A flowchart showing the basic procedure is shown in Figure 1.1.

Note: A divorce petition cannot be issued until one year has elapsed from the date of the marriage. This is an absolute bar, but note that it does not prevent the petitioner from presenting a petition based on matters that occurred before the expiration of the one-year period.

The first thing the petitioner needs to do is to decide upon the ground for divorce.

THE GROUND FOR DIVORCE

There is in fact only one ground for divorce – that the marriage has irretrievably broken down. However, the petitioner will have to prove irretrievable breakdown by proving one or more of the following:

a)   That the respondent has committed **adultery** *and* the petitioner finds it intolerable to live with the respondent (although for all practical purposes you do not really need to prove that you find it intolerable to live with the respondent). Note that adultery means the physical act of adultery – it is *not* sufficient to say that your spouse is having an affair or even that they are living with someone else. What this means in practice

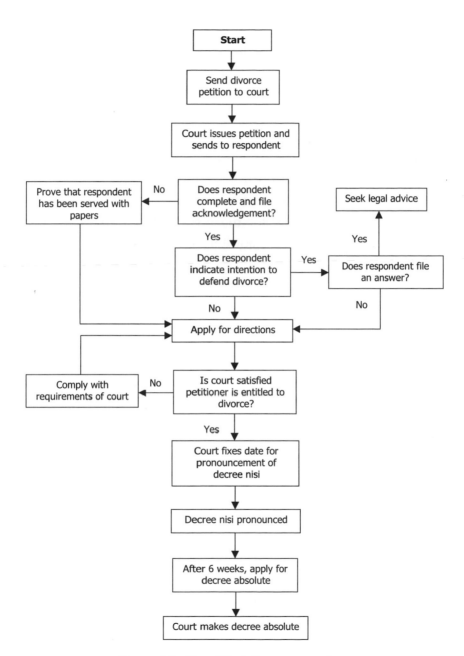

Figure 1.1   Simplified divorce procedure

is that the adultery will usually have to be admitted, unless a child has been born to the relationship. Accordingly, you will need to ensure that your spouse is prepared to admit the adultery for the purpose of the divorce (preferably in writing – see the example confession statement in Appendix 1), before issuing proceedings. If you issue divorce proceedings on the basis of adultery and are then unable to prove that adultery, you will not be able to proceed with the divorce. Note also that you cannot rely upon your spouse's adultery if you and he or she live together for more than six months after you have found out about the adultery (unless the adultery is still continuing).

A common question is whether or not to name the other person involved in the adultery (the 'co-respondent'). There is no obligation to name the co-respondent and my advice is not to do so unless you want to claim costs against them. If the co-respondent is named then they will become a party to the proceedings and they will therefore have to be served with the divorce petition. Often, they will not acknowledge receipt of the petition and the petitioner will then have to go to the trouble and expense of proving that the co-respondent has received it – see the section below on service of the papers. You should therefore think very carefully before naming the co-respondent.

b) That the respondent has behaved in such a way that the petitioner cannot reasonably be expected to live with the respondent (**unreasonable behaviour**).

Note:
1   A period or periods of living together after the last incident of unreasonable behaviour will be disregarded if the

length of that period or those periods was six months or less. In other words, if you are still living with your spouse the petition should be issued within six months of the last incident of unreasonable behaviour.

2   Unreasonable behaviour does not need to include violence – it can be any behaviour that you consider to have been unreasonable.

3   It is preferable not to mention children in allegations of unreasonable behaviour, if possible.

4   It is *not* sufficient to say that you and your spouse have 'drifted apart' or similar. There must be some element of fault on the part of your spouse.

5   Allegations of unreasonable behaviour should preferably be in concise numbered sub-paragraphs, including the first incident, the worst incident and the most recent incident. For more information, see the section on drafting the petition below and the example petition in Appendix 1.

c) That the respondent has deserted the petitioner for a continuous period of at least two years immediately preceding the presentation of the divorce petition (**two years' desertion**). You can safely ignore this one – desertion is extremely rare, and I have not come across a divorce petition based upon it in more than 20 years of doing divorce work.

d) That the parties have lived apart for a continuous period of at least two years immediately preceding the presentation of the divorce petition (**two years' separation**) *and* the respondent consents to the divorce.

Note:

1   That 'separation' usually means living in two entirely separate households. It is possible to be living separately albeit under the same roof, but this means completely separate, including sleeping separately, cooking and washing separately, and having separate financial arrangements.

2   That any period not exceeding six months or periods not exceeding six months in total that you resume living with your spouse will not prevent a divorce on this basis, but that period or those periods will be added to the total. For example, if you separate and then live together for three months, you will not be able to divorce on this basis until at least two years and three months have elapsed since the original date of separation.

3   Obviously, you will need to check that your spouse will consent, before issuing divorce proceedings on this basis. If you issue the divorce and your spouse does not then consent, you will not be able to proceed.

e) That the parties have lived apart for a continuous period of at least five years immediately preceding the presentation of the divorce petition (**five years' separation**) – without requiring the respondent's consent. Note that the same principles regarding separation and resumption of cohabitation as under paragraph (d) (1) and (2) apply. Note, though, that if the divorce is on the basis of five years' separation the respondent can oppose the divorce on the basis of 'grave financial or other hardship'. It is therefore important that financial arrangements are considered (or preferably agreed) before issuing a divorce petition on this basis.

THE PETITION

The next thing you will need to decide is which court to use. Divorces are dealt with by county courts, but not all county courts deal with divorce. For details of how to find your local divorce county court, see Appendix 4. Note that you do not have to use your nearest court – you may issue proceedings in any divorce county court. However, if the court is some distance from the matrimonial home then the respondent may request a transfer to the local court, especially if it is necessary to attend court for a hearing. The court will normally agree to such a request, which will cause a delay whilst the papers are transferred to the local court.

Once you have decided upon the basis of the divorce and which court to use, you can begin drafting the divorce petition. It is important that the petition is drafted correctly, as errors in it can at best cause further expense and delay while it is amended, or at worse they can make the document invalid, with the result that you have to start over again.

Now look at the example divorce petition in Appendix 1. The document essentially comprises five parts: the heading; the main body, in numbered paragraphs; the prayer (a throwback to when divorces were dealt with by ecclesiastical courts), which sets out what you are asking for from the court; the signature section; and the backsheet. With the exception of five-year separation divorces (see below), most divorce petitions contain the same sections and paragraphs.

The following deals with each section of the petition in turn.

The heading

Insert the name of the court (delete 'Principal Registry', if the divorce is not being issued there (if it is, delete the words 'In the [blank] County Court'). Leave the space after 'No.' blank – this is where the court will insert the case number. Insert your current full name after the words 'This petition is issued by', then insert the full current name of your spouse after the words 'The other party to the marriage is'.

The main body

The numbering of the following paragraphs corresponds with the numbering of the paragraphs in the main body of the petition:

1   The first paragraph sets out the details of the marriage, which must comply with the details set out in the marriage certificate (if you do not have the certificate see the section below regarding filing the papers with the court, for details of how to obtain a certified copy). You will need to insert the date of the marriage, the full names of both parties at the time of the marriage (petitioner first) and the place of the marriage. Be careful with the place of the marriage – the wording *must* be the same as in the marriage certificate (make sure you don't misspell 'Regis<u>te</u>r Office'!).

(1a) If you have changed your name since the date of the marriage (for example, by signing a change of name deed or by retaining a maiden name) you should state and explain this here, for example, 'Since the date of the marriage the name of the petitioner has changed by deed and he/she is now known as . . .' or 'Since the date of the marriage the name of the petitioner has changed as she retained her maiden name and is known as . . .'.

(1b) You should state similar details in respect of the respondent's name, if you believe it has changed since the date of the marriage.

2   State the last address at which you and your spouse last lived together as husband and wife.

3   This paragraph is required in order to show the court that it has jurisdiction to deal with the divorce, rather than a court in another country. This can cause some confusion but in the vast majority of cases it is quite straightforward, especially if both parties have always lived in England and Wales. The terms 'habitually resident' and 'domiciled' are used in what follows. 'Habitually resident' means what it says, and the country in which you are 'domiciled' is essentially the country in which you live, or would be living if you were not (temporarily) living where you are currently – i.e. the country to which you intend to return, having not emigrated on a permanent basis. With this in mind, you will need to insert whichever of the following paragraphs applies:

a)   'The petitioner and respondent are both habitually resident in England and Wales.'

b)   'The petitioner and respondent were last habitually resident in England and Wales and the petitioner [or the respondent] still resides there.'

c)   'The respondent is habitually resident in England and
      Wales.'

d)   'The petitioner is habitually resident in England and
      Wales and has resided there for at least one year
      immediately prior to the presentation of this petition.'
      Followed by the address or addresses where you lived
      during that year and the length of time you lived at each
      address.

e)   'The petitioner is domiciled and habitually resident in
      England and Wales and has resided there for at least
      six months immediately prior to the presentation of the
      petition.' Followed by the address or addresses where
      you lived during those six months and the length of
      time you lived at each address.

f)   'The petitioner and the respondent are both domiciled
      in England and Wales.'

If you are in any doubt which, if any, of the above paragraphs
applies to you then you should take advice – a Citizens Advice
Bureau (CAB) should be able to help (for details of how to
find your nearest CAB, see Appendix 2).

4   State the occupation and residence address of both parties, as
      at the date of the petition. If either party is not working then
      just state that they are 'unemployed'. It is also acceptable to use
      the terms 'househusband' or 'housewife' as an occupation, if
      appropriate. If you do not wish to disclose your address, for
      example because your spouse has been violent towards you
      and you do not want them to know your whereabouts, then
      you will need to ask the court for permission to omit your

address from the petition. This is done by filing with the petition a short affidavit setting out the reasons for omitting your address. If the application is granted, the petition may proceed and you may omit your address from any further documents filed in the proceedings.

5   For each child who is a child of both parties, or treated as a child of the family (see the section on Arrangements for Children below), state the child's full name (including surname) and their date of birth, unless they are over 18 (in which case state 'over 18'). If a child is aged 16 or 17, state whether they are at school/college, training for work or working full time. If there are no children, simply delete the word 'except'.

6   Where there are other children born to the wife during the marriage, their full name (including surname) and their date of birth, unless they are over 18 (in which case state 'over 18') should be inserted. If you are the husband, the paragraph should read: 'No other child, now living, has been born to the respondent during the marriage (so far as is known to the petitioner) except' – then state the details. If you are the wife, the paragraph should read: 'No other child, now living, has been born to the petitioner during the marriage except' – then state the details. In either case, if there are no children, simply delete the word 'except'. If there is a dispute over whether a living child is a child of the family, insert an additional paragraph: 'The petitioner alleges that [name of child] is [not] a child of the family'.

7   If there are or have been no other court proceedings with reference to the marriage (or to any child of the family) or between the petitioner and respondent with reference to any property of either or both of them, then leave this

paragraph as it is in the example. If there are or have been any such proceedings, add the word 'except' to the end of the paragraph and state the name of the court involved, the nature of the proceedings and details (including dates) of any court orders. If the proceedings related to the marriage itself, state whether you and the respondent resumed cohabitation after any order was made. If any proceedings relating to the marriage are still continuing in another country then their details will go in paragraph 9, so you can simply state 'except as set out in paragraph 9 below'.

8   If there are or have been any proceedings in the Child Support Agency, add the word 'except' to the end of the paragraph and then give the date of the application to the Agency and details of the child support calculation made.

9   If there are any continuing foreign court proceedings relating to the marriage, add the word 'except' to the end of the paragraph, then give details of the country, the court, the date the proceedings began, the names of the parties, details of any orders made and the date of any future hearing. (If there are any such proceedings then the court will decide whether you may proceed with your petition before those proceedings have been decided.)

10   If the divorce is based on five years' separation then you must state here whether an agreement or arrangement has been made or is proposed to be made between the parties for the support of the petitioner or respondent or any child of the family. If so, set out details of the agreement/arrangement. This paragraph should be deleted or omitted if the divorce is not based on five years' separation.

11   This paragraph sets out the ground for divorce and should not be altered.

12   Here you will need to set out the fact that you are relying upon to show that the marriage has irretrievably broken down, as follows:

(i)   **Adultery**: 'The respondent has committed adultery with [a man] [a woman] [or – if you wish to name the co-respondent insert their name and afterwards the words '(hereinafter called the 'co-respondent)'] and the petitioner finds it intolerable to live with the respondent.'

(ii) **Unreasonable behaviour**: 'The respondent has behaved in such a way that the petitioner cannot reasonably be expected to live with the respondent.'

(iii) **Desertion**: 'The respondent has deserted the petitioner for a continuous period of at least two years immediately preceding the presentation of this petition.'

(iv) **Two years' separation**: 'The parties to the marriage have lived apart for a continuous period of at least two years immediately preceding the presentation of the petition and the respondent consents to a decree being granted.'

(v)   **Five years' separation**: 'The parties to the marriage have lived apart for a continuous period of at least five years immediately preceding the presentation of the petition.'

Note that, save for detailing the co-respondent in a petition based upon adultery, the wording of these paragraphs should not be altered.

13   Here you will need to give brief particulars of the fact relied upon to show that the marriage has irretrievably broken down, as follows:

(i)   **Adultery**: You should state the dates on which or the periods over which the adultery is alleged to have taken place, together with details of the place or places at which it took place. Usually the petitioner will not have this information, but it is acceptable to state something like this: 'Since about December 2007 at an address or addresses unknown to the petitioner the respondent has committed adultery with the said man/woman.'

(ii) **Unreasonable behaviour**: Set out, in numbered sub-paragraphs, *brief* details of the alleged behaviour, including any particular incidents, with dates and places. You do *not* need to write out a full history of the marriage, or even details of every incident. Keep it short – writing pages of allegations will only annoy the judge. In the unlikely event of the divorce being defended, you will have an opportunity to add to the allegations. A useful rule of thumb is to set out details of the first, worst and last incidents (although certain types of unreasonable behaviour can be of a continuous nature). The first incident will give an indication of how long the behaviour has been going on, the worst incident will give an indication of the seriousness of the behaviour, and the last incident should be within the last six months (see above). Remember, you need only say enough to satisfy the court that the marriage has irretrievably broken down, although if the allegations are on the weak side, then it may be necessary to give more detail. If possible, try not to mention the children in any allegations, as if you do then the respondent is more likely to object to the allegations, as they may have a bearing upon arrangements for the children. If you believe that your spouse has committed adultery but cannot prove it, then you may say that they had a relationship with that person but not that they committed adultery. For an example of unreasonable behaviour particulars, see the example petition in Appendix 1.

(iii) **Desertion**: Simply state the date when and the circumstances in which the desertion took place.

(iv) **Two or five years' separation**: Again, just state the date when and (if you wish) the circumstances in which the separation took place, for example: 'The parties separated on the 1st day of January 2008 and have not lived together since that date.'

The prayer

1 **The suit**: Here you are requesting the court to dissolve the marriage. Leave the wording exactly as shown in the example petition.

2 **Costs**: If you wish to make a claim that the respondent pay your costs, then leave this paragraph as shown in the example. If, in an adultery divorce, you have named the co-respondent and wish to also claim costs against them, then state 'co-respondent' as well as respondent. If you only want the respondent to pay part of your costs (perhaps because this has already been agreed – see below), then amend the paragraph accordingly, for example 'That the respondent may

be ordered to pay one half of the costs of this suit', or 'That the respondent may be ordered to pay the costs of this suit limited to the sum of £170'. Alternatively, you may only want to claim costs if the respondent should defend the divorce (see below – defended divorce proceedings can be extremely expensive, and such a claim may therefore dissuade the respondent from defending), in which case simply add the words 'if defended' to the end of the paragraph. If you do not wish to claim costs at all, then just delete this paragraph. Note that claiming costs is not appropriate in divorces based upon five years' separation.

3   **Ancillary relief**: This is the part of the petition that causes most confusion. 'Ancillary relief' means any financial/property claim against your spouse, and for full details you should refer to Chapter 4. The simplest rule is: if in doubt, include the claims. The reason for this is that by including the claims you give yourself the option of proceeding with the claims (thereby avoiding the 'remarriage trap' – see Chapter 4), but you do *not* have to proceed with the claims. (Note that if you do not include the claims in the petition then you will need the court's permission to proceed with them later.) You may, for example, have agreed all financial property matters with your spouse and simply want to include the claims so that they can be dismissed by the court in a consent order – again, see Chapter 4. The paragraph is divided into two sections – claims for yourself and claims for any children. Leave all the claims for yourself in, as set out in the example petition, although if you are asking for a property adjustment order you should give the address of the property concerned, and if you are asking for a pension sharing or attachment order you

should give details of the order you are seeking, if you know these. If there are any children, leave the claims for them in, although it is quite rare to proceed with any such claims – child maintenance (or 'periodical payments') is usually dealt with by the Child Support Agency if not agreed, unless this is one of the cases where the Agency cannot deal with the matter – see Chapter 3.

The signature section

Once the petition is complete, you should sign it beneath the prayer. Below that, insert the name and address of the respondent and (if named) the co-respondent. Below that, insert your address as the 'address for service' (i.e. the address to which all court papers for you will be sent). If you do not want the papers to be sent to your home address, for example because your spouse still lives there and you are afraid they may intercept them, or if the court has granted you permission to omit your address from the petition (see above) then you may give another address for service. Finally, beneath your address for service you should date the petition, preferably with the date that it is sent to the court or the date you file it with the court, if you attend the court to file it personally (see below).

The backsheet

The purpose of the backsheet is essentially to protect the document, the idea being that the petition is folded in half top to bottom, and the right-hand half contains all the details of the document. As will be seen from the example, the details comprise the court, a space for the case number, the parties' names, the title of the document ('Divorce Petition') and the full name and address of the petitioner. The backsheet always faces outwards, so that it can be read without opening the document.

ARRANGEMENTS FOR CHILDREN

Where there are children of the family under 16 or between 16 and 18 and undergoing education or training (who I will call 'relevant children'), the court has to be satisfied that proper arrangements are made for them, before allowing the divorce to proceed. Accordingly, where there are such children the petitioner will need to complete a statement of arrangements for children form, setting out details of the children and the arrangements, or proposed arrangements, for them.

Before going any further I need to explain the term 'children of the family'. This does not only include the children of both parties, but also any other children who are *treated as children of the family*, such as step children. Accordingly, their details will also have to be included in the statement of arrangements for children form. For children who have not been treated as children of the family, you will only need to give their names and dates of birth in section 3 of the form – see below.

The form is usually quite easy to complete, but there are some pitfalls, especially if your circumstances don't fit the questions on the form. Once you have read the 'To the petitioner' notes on the front, insert the court and parties' names. Give the details of all relevant children (see above) in section 3 on the second page, following the instructions. Section 4 (home details) is self-explanatory, although if the children do not live with you then you may not have all of this information. If this is the case, give as much information as you can and state 'not known' for any missing information. Note that the court is concerned about the children's primary residence, that is, where they spend most of their time, so there is no need to give details for the other parent's home just because they spend some nights there. If their time is shared equally between two households, state this and give details of both households.

Section 5 of the form (education and training details) is again pretty straightforward. Note that 'school' does not include nursery school, only primary school onwards. 'Special educational needs' in subsection (b) refers to any such needs identified by the school/college, so there is no need to mention minor problems, such as that a child is behind with their reading skills, unless the school has specifically stated that the child has special needs. Subsection (c) only needs to be completed if one or both of the parents is paying all or part of any fees. In subsection (d), you only really need to give details of any change in education arrangements if the child is being moved from one school to another (i.e. there is no need, for example, to state that the child will be going to secondary school next year), for example due to change of location or change from private to state school. If the child is simply in between schools (for example, having just left primary school), then section 5 should contain details of the next school that the child will be attending.

Section 6 (childcare details) is another one that could cause problems if the children don't live with you and you don't have all of the information, but give as many details as you can, as the court may raise a query if it appears that any children are not looked after by an adult all of the time. If a relative (for example, a grandparent) looks after the children, give their relationship to the children. If a childminder is used, give their details at subsections (c) and (d), as appropriate, but there is no need to go into every detail, for example babysitting arrangements.

Section 7 (maintenance) is designed to be completed by the recipient of child maintenance, so will need to be amended if you are the payer, in which case tick 'Yes' at subsection (a) and state below 'I am paying £x per week' etc., and tick 'No' to both questions at subsection (e), if maintenance has not been agreed. If you are the recipient and maintenance has not been agreed, you should tick 'Yes' to the second question at subsection (e), to indicate that you intend to apply for child support, unless (unusually) the Child Support Agency does not have jurisdiction (see the section 'When the CSA/C-MEC is not available', in Chapter 3).

Section 8 (details for contact with the children) is again designed to be completed by the primary carer of the children, so will need to be amended if you are not the primary carer, to show what contact you are having. If that is the case and you are not happy with the contact you are having, state this at subsection (c) and set out what contact you seek. If contact arrangements are agreed but are flexible (i.e. no fixed arrangement for contact on specific days), then complete the section with details of how much contact takes place on average.

Section 9 (details of health) is self-explanatory but, as the notes state, only give details of serious issues. Minor issues, such as needing glasses for 'normal' eyesight problems or mild asthma, do not need to be detailed.

You should already be aware if there are any matters to be included in section 10 (details of care and other court proceedings). Note that you only need answer 'Yes' to subsection (b) if the children are *currently* on the Child Protection Register, and that if there has been has been a court order relating to the children, a copy of the order should be attached to the form.

In Part III of the form it asks whether, if you and your spouse do not agree about arrangements for the children, you would agree to discuss the matter with him/her and a conciliator. Here, 'conciliator' really means 'mediator' (see Chapter 6). You should answer 'Yes', unless you have strong reasons to object to mediation, for example if your spouse has been violent towards you. Otherwise, even if arrangements are agreed, I would still suggest answering 'Yes' to this question, in case there is any dispute in the future. When the form has been completed and you are satisfied with the contents, sign and date the declaration.

Part IV of the form is for the respondent to sign, if they agree with the arrangements set out in the form – see below.

BEFORE FILING WITH THE COURT

In order to avoid potentially expensive problems down the line, details of the allegations in the petition should be shown to your spouse and, if possible, agreed. For example, if the respondent takes exception to an allegation of their unreasonable behaviour they may choose to defend the divorce (see below), which would result in considerable expense and delay. I would recommend sending them a copy of the whole petition, as this may show up any errors in the document, which would otherwise involve a costly application to the court to have the petition amended after it is issued. As indicated above, if you need the respondent to admit adultery or to consent to the divorce, these things will need to be agreed before the papers are filed, in any event.

You may also reach an agreement with your spouse as to who will pay the costs of the divorce or as to how those costs may be divided between the parties.

The statement of arrangements for children form should also be sent to your spouse, for them to sign if they agree with the arrangements that you propose. If they do not agree, the form can still be filed with the court signed only by the petitioner, although the respondent will be given the opportunity to file their own form and the court may well then direct that the divorce cannot proceed until matters have been resolved – hence arrangements should be agreed if possible before issuing the divorce – see Chapter 2.

FILING WITH THE COURT

The documents that have to be filed with the court are:

1   The original, signed, divorce petition.

2   One extra copy of the petition for every other party to the proceedings, so one copy if you have not named a co-respondent and two copies if you have.

3   The original, signed, statement of arrangements for children form, if one has been prepared – see above.

4   A copy of the statement of arrangements for children form.

5   Your original marriage certificate, or a certified copy (*not* a photocopy). If you do not have your original marriage certificate then you will have to obtain a certified copy from the Register Office where the marriage took place or,

if you were not married in a Register Office, the Office local to where the marriage took place, or from the church, if the Register Office does not yet have the certificate. There is a fee of £7 payable for a certified copy marriage certificate. Note that if you were married abroad and your marriage certificate is in a foreign language, then you will also need an English translation, certified by a notary public.

6   Copies of any court orders referred to in the divorce petition.

You should retain a copy of every document that you file, including the marriage certificate.

You will need to pay the court fee of £300 when filing the divorce papers. As with all court fees, cheques should be made payable to 'H.M. Courts Service'. If you are on a low income, then you may be entitled to a fee exemption. To apply for a fee exemption you will need to complete a fee exemption form, which you can obtain from the court office.

The divorce papers and fee can be filed either by post or by attending the court office personally.

Note that, as mentioned above, a divorce petition cannot be issued until one year has elapsed from the date of the marriage. Accordingly, if you have not yet been married for a year then you will have to wait until one year and a day after the date of the marriage before filing the divorce papers (which should be dated with the date they are filed).

SERVICE OF THE PAPERS

Divorce papers must, if possible, be served upon the respondent. The papers to be served comprise a copy of the divorce petition, a copy of the statement of arrangements for children form and an acknowledgement of service form and notice of proceedings, which will be provided by the court. In the first instance, the papers will be sent to the respondent by the court by post (at the address you gave for the respondent in the petition), unless specified otherwise.

It will be necessary to prove to the satisfaction of the court that the respondent has received the divorce papers. Obviously, this will not be a problem if the respondent completes the acknowledgement of service form and returns it to the court (see below), but what if the respondent fails to do this? The next step depends upon the circumstances.

If you know that your spouse has received the divorce papers, because they have told you so, or because you have seen them in their possession, you could use that as evidence that they have received them. You can then apply for an order that service of the petition be presumed to have taken place, known as 'deemed service'. The application involves drafting a short affidavit setting out why you maintain that your spouse has received the papers, and filing it with the court, together with a £40 court fee. If the court is satisfied that your spouse has received the papers, it will make an order for deemed service, and you can then apply for the divorce to proceed – see below. An example affidavit in support of an application for deemed service can be found in Appendix 1.

If, on the other hand, you do not have such evidence, then the next step will be to arrange for the papers to be handed to your spouse personally. You could arrange for a professional 'process server' to give your spouse the papers in person. However, this will involve extra costs. You may get these costs back if you succeed in your claim that your spouse should meet your costs of the divorce and those costs are paid. If the process server is successful, then they will swear an affidavit of service, which you may use as proof of service. Alternatively, you may request that the court bailiff serve the papers. This involves filling in a request form (available from the court) and paying a fee of £30, but court bailiffs are generally far less strenuous than process servers in their efforts to effect service, which could be a problem if the respondent tries to evade service. If the bailiff does effect service, then they will invite the respondent to sign an indorsement of service, which is used as proof of service. Lastly, you may know of someone who could serve the papers for you, which would keep the costs down. You cannot hand the papers to your spouse yourself.

As a last resort, it is sometimes possible to get an order from the court that service should take place by the papers being sent to someone other than your spouse, such as a member of their family (known as 'substituted service'). However, the courts generally need to be persuaded that it is impossible to carry out service in any other way, and it will still be necessary to prove that that person has received the papers.

What if you simply do not know the whereabouts of the respondent or of any way to effect service of the divorce papers upon them? In this case, you can apply to the court for an order dispensing with service of the papers upon them. However, the court will only make such an order if it is satisfied that you have made every reasonable effort to trace the respondent. You will need to swear an affidavit detailing those efforts, which include making enquiries of the respondent's friends, relatives, former employers and bank. A form of affidavit is available from the court office and a £40 fee is payable on the application. An example affidavit is not included in the appendix as it is in a simple question and answer format and should be quite straightforward to complete. (These applications are often made simultaneously with the filing of the divorce petition, rather than afterwards.)

Note that if you need the respondent to admit adultery or to consent to the divorce in their acknowledgement, then there is of course no point in going to the expense of proving service as you will still not be able to proceed with the divorce – this is why it is essential that these matters are dealt with *before* the divorce proceedings are issued.

THE ACKNOWLEDGEMENT OF SERVICE

If you are the respondent to the divorce you will receive a copy of the divorce petition, a copy of the statement of arrangements for children form (if applicable), an acknowledgement of service form (which you must complete and return to the court) and a notice of proceedings, which explains what you must do. Read the notice before completing the acknowledgement form – this will tell you, amongst other things, how long you have to complete the acknowledgement and return it to the court (usually eight days, including the day of receipt, unless you live abroad). Do not delay returning the acknowledgement as this can add to the costs (as the notice states), as the petitioner may then go to the expense of proving service – see above.

The form of the acknowledgement of service will depend upon the basis of the divorce. If the divorce is on the basis of adultery or unreasonable behaviour, it will look like the example in Appendix 1. If it is on a separation basis, it will include other questions, as mentioned below, and the numbering of the questions will differ from the numbering in the example, and those used below. As will be seen, the acknowledgement is essentially in a simple question and answer format and most of it is quite straightforward to complete, but certain sections can cause difficulty so the sections are explained below. Note that it should be completed using black ink.

All forms of acknowledgement include questions 1, 1A, 1B and 1C. Obviously, question 1 should be answered 'Yes' – if you have not received a copy of the petition, then request this from the court. As to question 1A, you can complete the requested details, but if you want the divorce to be dealt with in another country then you should really seek legal advice, as this can involve complex issues of law that are beyond the scope of this book. For help in answering questions 1B and 1C, see above regarding completing paragraph 3 of the main body of the divorce petition.

Questions 2 and 3 should be completely straightforward – the date you put in the answer to question 2 determines how long you have to complete the acknowledgement and return it to the court, as mentioned above.

Question 4 is the most important in the acknowledgement, where you state whether or not you intend to defend the divorce. If you are minded to defend, then first read the section below on defended divorce and cross petitions. If you do want to defend, then answer 'Yes'. If you do not wish to defend then answer 'No'. In a divorce based upon unreasonable behaviour, you may not want to defend but you may take exception to the allegations of your unreasonable behaviour in the petition. If these are not too serious, you can answer something like 'No, but I do not accept the allegations of unreasonable behaviour', in order to reserve the right to object to those allegations, should the petitioner try to use them in connection with matters relating to children or finances. If the allegations are serious, for example they specifically include allegations of unreasonable behaviour towards the children, or if they allege that you have committed a serious criminal offence, then you should consult a solicitor, as you may need to defend the divorce, unless the petitioner agrees to amend the petition (see below) by deleting the allegations.

Question 5 relates to adultery divorces only (it can be ignored otherwise) and is where you state whether or not you admit the adultery. Obviously, you can only admit it if you have committed it – don't be tempted to admit adultery that hasn't occurred, just to get the divorce through. Hopefully, the issue will have been sorted out with the petitioner before the proceedings were issued (see the sections above on the Ground for Divorce and Before Filing with the Court) but if it has not be aware that admitting adultery is likely to make you liable to pay the petitioner's costs, if they have included a claim for costs in the petition. If this is the case, you may wish to write to the petitioner or their solicitor, informing them that you will only admit the adultery if they drop their claim for costs (make sure the letter is headed 'without prejudice'), as they will usually only be able to prove the adultery (and therefore proceed with the divorce) if you admit it – be aware, though, that the petitioner could then amend the petition to the basis of unreasonable behaviour, so as to be able to claim their costs.

Unless the petitioner has not included a claim for costs in the petition (see the section above on the prayer in the petition – if there is no claim simply answer 'not applicable'), or the issue of who will pay the costs was agreed before the proceedings were commenced (in which case, answer appropriately, for example, 'I agree to pay the petitioner's costs, limited to £500 including VAT').

Question 6 does require some explanation. Costs orders are made against the party who is found to be at fault for the breakdown of the marriage. Accordingly, if the divorce is based upon your adultery or unreasonable behaviour, then you are likely to have a costs order made against you. It is therefore pointless to say anything in the answer to this question that is not relevant to the issue of fault, such as that you didn't want the divorce or that you can't afford to pay (although this may be relevant to the amount of the costs and the time you are given to pay). Generally, the best you can say is that the breakdown of the marriage was the petitioner's fault or equally their fault. If you do object to paying the costs, then, if the petitioner still proceeds with their claim (see the next section), the court will usually do one of three things: make the order (most likely), make no order, or require the parties to attend court when the decree nisi is pronounced (see below) to argue the issue – the court will then make a decision, after hearing from both parties. In a divorce based upon two years' separation, you obviously have complete control over the issue of costs, as the petitioner cannot proceed with the divorce without your consent – simply inform the petitioner or their solicitor that you will not consent unless they drop their claim for costs or unless the costs are shared. In a divorce based upon five years' separation it is not appropriate for the respondent to be ordered to pay costs, as there is no fault involved – in such a case, you should state that it is not appropriate, in the answer to question 6.

Question 7 relates to the statement of arrangements for children form – see the section on this above. Hopefully, the petitioner will have sent you the form before the proceedings were issued, you will have agreed the arrangements for the children and signed the form – if so, answering question 7 will be straightforward. Otherwise, if you only have minor disagreements with the proposals set out in the form, state these in your answer to question 7(c). If you have major disagreements, then you should obtain a form of your own from the court, complete it and return it to the court with the acknowledgement.

Answer 'Not applicable' to question 8 – you don't have another husband/wife, do you?

As mentioned above, the acknowledgement form in separation divorce cases has extra questions. These are:

1   *Do you consent to a decree being granted?* This of course only relates to two-year separation divorce cases. Note the discussion above regarding the issue of costs.

2   *Do you intend to oppose the grant of a decree on the ground that the divorce will result in grave financial or other hardship to you and that in all the circumstances it would be wrong to dissolve the marriage?* This only relates to five-year separation divorce cases. As mentioned above in the section on the ground for divorce, the respondent in such a case can oppose the divorce on the basis of 'grave financial or other hardship', for example loss of a widow's pension if the marriage is dissolved. If you think this may apply to you, then you should consult a solicitor. Note that if you answer 'Yes', then you must, within 28 days of receiving the petition, file with the court an answer to the petition (see the section below on defended divorce), setting out details of the financial hardship you will suffer and requesting that the divorce petition be dismissed.

3   *In the event of a decree being granted on the basis of two years'*
    separation coupled with the respondent's consent, or five years'
    separation, do you intend to apply to the Court for it to consider your
    financial position as it will be after the divorce? This is similar to
    the previous paragraph, but here you are not asking for the
    divorce to be stopped, merely that it be delayed until finances
    have been resolved. Again, loss of pension rights is the most
    likely reason to request this. If you are in any doubt whether
    you should ask for the divorce to be delayed then, again, you
    should consult a solicitor. Note that if you answer 'Yes' then
    you will also have to complete and file a 'Form B' (obtainable
    from the court), followed by a 'Form E' – see Chapter 4. Note
    also that answering 'No' does not prevent you from later
    applying to the court for a financial/property settlement
    (ancillary relief).

Finally, you must complete and sign the first signature section of
the acknowledgement (you can ignore the second section if you
do not have a solicitor) – section 9(a) of the example. You must
give an address for service, that is, the address to which all court
papers will be sent. This does not necessarily have to be your
place of residence.

Once you have completed the acknowledgement of service, take a
copy for yourself and send the original to the court, at the address
at the bottom of the second page. The court will then send a copy
of the acknowledgement to the petitioner or their solicitor.

APPLYING FOR THE DIVORCE TO PROCEED

If the respondent has confirmed in his or her acknowledgement of service form that they do not intend to defend the divorce (see below), or if the respondent's time for filing the acknowledgement has expired (and the petitioner can prove that the respondent has received the papers) then the petitioner can apply for the divorce to proceed. The application is made by filing with the court an application for directions for trial form together with an affidavit in support of the petition. Many courts will send these documents to the petitioner with the copy of the respondent's acknowledgement of service, but see also Appendix 1.

As will be seen from Appendix 1, the application for directions for trial is a very simple form that essentially only requires completion of the heading, signing and dating.

The exact contents of the affidavit in support of the petition will depend upon the basis of the divorce. Leaving aside desertion, there is one affidavit for adultery divorces, one for unreasonable behaviour divorces and one for divorces on the basis of two or five years' separation (these two are essentially the same). An example of each can be found in Appendix 1. As will be seen, all of the affidavits have common paragraphs. The following explains the affidavit in support of adultery petition in detail, and then explains those paragraphs that are different in the other two affidavits. All three affidavits are in two parts: a question and answer section, followed by the body of the affidavit itself, where you confirm that the answers that you have given previously are true.

Affidavit in support of adultery petition

Refer to the example in Appendix 1.

Question 1: Always answer 'yes', obviously!

Question 2: Check through your petition and make sure that everything in it is still correct. If there is anything wrong in the petition, state it here. If you do not do so, then the district judge may pick it up when you apply for the divorce to proceed (see below) and may refuse to allow the divorce to proceed (you may then have to go to the trouble and expense of amending your petition – see the section below on Amended and Supplemental Petitions). Typical errors are in the spelling of names, addresses and the place of marriage. Do not try to add to the grounds for divorce, for example by alleging unreasonable behaviour as well as adultery, or to add to the allegations in the petition, as the court may then want you to amend the petition and re-serve it on the respondent. If you do not wish to alter the petition, simply answer 'No'.

Question 3: You will normally answer 'Yes' to this question, as your petition should not usually contain any statements that are not within your own knowledge.

Question 4: This is the first of the questions specific to adultery petitions. As you will normally be relying upon the respondent to admit the adultery, you should usually answer 'Because the respondent has admitted the adultery' or similar. If a child has been born to the respondent as a result of the adulterous relationship and you are using this to prove the adultery, then state it here – you may also wish to exhibit to the affidavit a copy of the child's birth certificate, giving the respondent as a parent. Note that simply stating that the respondent has been seeing someone else is *not* proof of adultery – see the section above on the ground for divorce.

Question 5: The importance of this question is that you cannot rely upon the adultery if you and your spouse lived together for more than six months after you found out about the adultery (unless the adultery is still continuing) – again, see the section above on the ground for divorce. Note that the relevant date is the date that you *found out* about the adultery, rather than the date that the adultery began. State the date here. If you are not sure about the exact date, state 'On about the [date]'.

Question 6: Always answer 'Yes' to this question – you cannot rely upon the adultery unless you also find it intolerable to live with the respondent.

Question 7: Again, this relates to the six-month rule referred to in question 5 above. Answer the question with the facts but make sure that the period is less than six months – if not then, if it is the case, state that the adultery is still continuing.

Question 8: This and the next two questions are the same in all three affidavits. Obviously, answer 'Yes' to this one.

Question 9: Again, check the statement of arrangements form before answering this one. It would also be useful to check what the respondent stated about the form in their acknowledgement of service – they may have picked up on any errors in the form. If anything does require alteration, state it here, otherwise simply answer 'No'.

Question 10: Like question 3, you will normally answer 'Yes' to this question.

We now move on to the body of the affidavit itself. Insert your full name, address (don't worry if you do not wish to disclose this to the respondent – they will not see the affidavit) and occupation. Paragraphs 1 and 2 then require no alteration. Paragraph 3 should be deleted if the respondent's acknowledgement of service was signed by a solicitor and not by the respondent, although it will normally be signed by the respondent in adultery divorces. If the respondent did sign it, put their signature in inverted commas after the words 'I identify the signature...' exactly as it appears on the acknowledgement, so if the respondent signed the acknowledgement 'J Smith', put that in paragraph 3, and, later in the paragraph, delete the word 'husband' or 'wife', as appropriate. You will then need to exhibit a copy of the respondent's acknowledgement of service to the affidavit. This is done by marking the top of the front of the copy with the letter 'A', or by attaching to the copy an 'exhibit note', on which is written: 'This is the exhibit marked "A" referred to in the affidavit of [name] sworn this [blank] day of [blank], before me [blank]'. The blanks will be filled in by the person before whom you swear the affidavit – see below.

Paragraph 4 of the affidavit is to be completed in a similar fashion where the respondent has signed a confession statement – see the section above on the ground for divorce. Again, a copy of the statement is exhibited to the affidavit. Note that if the respondent has indicated in their acknowledgement of service that they admit the adultery, and signed the acknowledgement, then there is little point in also exhibiting the confession statement. If you are not exhibiting a confession statement, then this paragraph can be deleted.

Paragraph 5 is for use where the respondent has signed the statement of arrangements for children form. If so, complete the paragraph in a similar way to the above and exhibit a copy of the statement to the affidavit. If there are no children, or if the respondent has not signed the statement, then delete this paragraph.

Paragraph 6 is to be used where you wish to exhibit any other document upon which you intend to rely, such as a child's birth certificate (see above). Write out the paragraph in a similar fashion to the previous paragraphs and exhibit a copy of the document to the affidavit.

Lastly, paragraph 7 sets out what you are asking the court to do, that is, to grant a decree (nisi) dissolving the marriage and, if appropriate, to order the respondent and/or co-respondent to pay your costs of the divorce (see the section above on the prayer in the divorce petition). If you do not wish to claim costs, then delete the words in square brackets. If you only wish to claim costs against the respondent, then delete the words 'co-respondent'. If the amount of the costs has been agreed, or you only wish to claim part of the costs, then amend the paragraph as appropriate, for example 'and to order the respondent to pay [£500 towards] [one half of] the costs of this suit'.

You then just need to complete the backsheet to the affidavit in the usual way.

Affidavit in support of behaviour petition

Refer to the example in Appendix 1.

Question 1: This is worded differently from question 1 in the adultery affidavit but is essentially the same and should therefore also be answered 'Yes'.

Questions 2 and **3**: These are exactly the same as in the adultery affidavit.

Question 4: You don't need to worry too much about how you answer this question, as it will have little bearing upon whether you are entitled to the divorce. If the respondent's behaviour has affected your health, give brief details. If it has not, answer: 'The respondent's behaviour has not affected my health'. You may have mentioned the effect of the respondent's behaviour upon your health in your petition, in which case you can answer something like: 'The respondent's behaviour has not affected my health, save as stated in my petition'.

Question 5: This and question 6 is relevant to the six month rule – see the ground for divorce section above. Answer 'Yes' or 'No' to the first part and, if you answered 'No', then put the date of the last incident of the respondent's unreasonable behaviour in the second part.

Question 6: You must show that you and the respondent have not lived together for more than six months since the date of the last incident of the respondent's unreasonable behaviour. If you have not lived at the same address as the respondent since that date (or if no date was given in the answer to question 5, since the date of the petition), then answer 'No' to the first part of this question and ignore the second part. Note, however, that you can still be counted as living apart albeit at the same address if you are really living completely separately from the respondent, as far as possible.

Accordingly, if you had to answer 'Yes' to the first part of the question then you will need to complete the second part to show that you were living completely separately. Obviously, the more separate the arrangements, the more likely that the court will find that you are living completely separately, so it is preferable if you are sleeping in separate rooms, cooking separately and not paying each other's bills.

Questions 7 to 9: These are the same as questions 8 to 10 of the adultery affidavit.

The body of the affidavit itself is similar to the body of the adultery affidavit, save that instead of providing for the exhibiting of a confession statement it provides (at paragraph 4) for the exhibiting of a medical report, in those (rare) cases where the petitioner wishes to rely upon such a report as evidence of the effect of the respondent's behaviour upon their health.

Affidavit in support of separation petition

Refer to the example in Appendix 1.

Questions 1 to 3: These are exactly the same as in the adultery affidavit.

Question 4: Insert the date of the separation, exactly as it appeared in your petition.

Question 5: The answer to this question is not particularly important, so you don't need to worry too much about what you say here – you certainly do not need to give detailed reasons for the separation. Something like: 'The respondent and I were not compatible' will suffice.

Question 6: Again, you need not worry too much about how you answer this question. Something as simple as: 'At the time of the separation, in the above circumstances' (referring to your answer to the previous question) is sufficient.

Question 7: This question is important, as your answer will prove that you and the respondent have lived separately for the requisite period (two or five years). You should therefore include as many details as you can of your, and the respondent's, addresses, with dates, since the date of the separation. Make sure that there are no gaps in the dates, and if you are not sure of an exact date put the month, the year or 'about [date]'. Similarly, if you do not know an address, give as much detail as you can, for example the road or town in which the respondent lived.

Question 8: This relates to the six-month rule relating to separation cases, referred to in the above section on the Ground for Divorce. To reiterate, any period not exceeding six months or periods not exceeding six months in total that you resume living with the respondent after the date of the separation will not prevent a divorce on the basis of two or five years' separation, but that period or those periods will be added to the total. If there have been any such periods, set them out in the answer, but make sure that they don't total more than six months and that they have been added to the two- or five-year period.

Questions 9 to 11: These are the same as questions 8 to 10 of the adultery affidavit.

The body of the affidavit itself is very similar to the body of the behaviour affidavit, although there should be no need to exhibit a medical report. As to paragraph 6, remember that claiming costs is not appropriate in divorces based upon five years' separation.

Once you have completed the affidavit, you will need to get it sworn. This can be done either at the divorce court or in front of a solicitor (not belonging to the firm acting for the respondent). If you take it to the court, the court office will be open from 10am to 4pm Mondays to Fridays and they will not charge a fee for this service. If you take the affidavit to a solicitor, you will be charged a fee of £5, plus £2 for each exhibit (don't forget to take the exhibits with you when you get it sworn!).

Once the affidavit has been sworn it should be filed with the court together with any exhibits (keep copies for yourself) and the application for directions form. There is no fee to pay.

THE DECREE NISI

After you apply for the divorce to proceed, the matter will go before a district judge – this is usually the only time a judge considers the papers in an undefended divorce. The district judge will consider three things: whether you are entitled to the divorce, who should pay the costs (if you have claimed costs in your petition) and whether they are satisfied about arrangements for any children. I will deal with each of these in turn.

If the district judge is satisfied that you are entitled to the divorce, then they will certify this and fix a date for the pronouncement of the decree nisi – see below. If the district judge is not satisfied that you are entitled to the divorce, then they may give you the opportunity to file further evidence with the court, possibly by way of an affidavit dealing with the issue or by requiring you to amend the petition – see the section below regarding amended petitions. Alternatively, if there is a serious problem then the district judge will remove the case from the special procedure list, which essentially means that the divorce cannot be dealt with on the papers alone and you will have to apply for a hearing to be fixed, at which the court will give directions as to how the matter is to proceed – in such a situation, you should consult a solicitor.

If the district judge certifies that you are entitled to the divorce then, if you have claimed costs in your petition, they will consider that claim. If they are satisfied that you are entitled to the costs (for example where the respondent does not object to paying), they will include a statement to that effect in the certificate. If they are not satisfied, then the parties will usually either be given the opportunity to file further evidence on the issue of costs (that is, explain why the respondent should/should not pay) or will be required to attend court when the decree nisi is pronounced to argue the issue (if the respondent does not attend, then the court will simply order them to pay the costs). For further information on the issue of costs, see Chapter 7.

The third matter that the district judge will consider is the arrangements for any children. If they are satisfied with the arrangements, they will certify that the court need not take any action regarding the children. If they are not satisfied, then the court will give directions as to what needs to be done. These may include the parties filing further evidence relating to the arrangements for the children, that a welfare report be prepared or that the parties attend the court. The court may also direct that the divorce should not be finalised until it is satisfied with the arrangements for the children. For further information regarding arrangements for children, and the types of orders that the court can make, see Chapter 2.

If the district judge is satisfied that you are entitled to the divorce, then you will receive notification of the date for the pronouncement of the decree nisi. The decree nisi is pronounced in open court but there is usually no need to attend. Normally, the only time an attendance is required is when one of the parties objects to the court making an order for costs – see above. The court will post the decree nisi to you after it is pronounced.

THE DECREE ABSOLUTE – AND WHEN
TO APPLY FOR IT

The court will not make the decree absolute automatically after six weeks have elapsed since the pronouncement of the decree nisi – it has to be applied for, usually by the petitioner but occasionally by the respondent.

The petitioner can apply for the decree absolute after six weeks have elapsed from the date of the pronouncement of the decree nisi. Note the word 'after' – the application cannot be made before six weeks have elapsed even if it reaches the court after that date. The simplest rule of thumb is don't make the application until six weeks *and one day* after the decree nisi. The application is made by filing with the court a simple notice of application for decree nisi to be made absolute form (see Appendix 1), together with the £40 court fee.

When the application for decree absolute is filed, the court will check its records to ensure that it can make the decree absolute. The following does not include everything the court checks, but some points are worth noting before filing the application so that it is not wasted:

1   A decree nisi can be set aside (or *rescinded*) in several different circumstances, for example on the application of the respondent to a two years' separation divorce where they were misled by the petitioner in giving their consent to the divorce, where the decree was issued in error or where a reconciliation has been effected. The court will not allow the decree nisi to be made absolute where an application for rescission of the decree nisi is pending.

2   The decree nisi cannot be made absolute where the court has not yet considered the arrangements for any children or has directed that the divorce should not be finalised until it is satisfied with the arrangements for the children – see above.

3   As mentioned above in the section on completing the acknowledgement of service, in a divorce based upon two or five years' separation the respondent can make an application asking that the divorce be delayed until finances have been resolved. Obviously, the decree nisi cannot be made absolute until any such application has been dealt with.

Whether or not the divorce is based upon two or five years' separation, you may wish to delay applying for the decree absolute until finances have been resolved. In fact, this occurs in the majority of cases. The primary reason for this is again loss of pension rights when the divorce is finalised. If you are in any doubt as to whether you should delay finalising the divorce until the financial settlement, then obviously you should not apply and you should seek legal advice.

Sometimes there can be a long delay between the pronouncement of the decree nisi and the application for the decree absolute, especially if it has taken a long time to sort out the financial settlement. If more than 12 months have elapsed since the decree nisi then, in addition to the application for decree absolute, you will also need to lodge a letter with the court stating:

1   The reasons for the delay, for example, that you were waiting until a financial/property settlement had been reached.

2   Whether you and the respondent have lived with each other since the decree nisi and, if so, between what dates – remember the rules on living together, mentioned above.

3   Whether, if you are the wife you have, or if you are the husband you have reason to believe that your wife has, given birth to any child since the decree nisi. If so, you must give details and state whether or not it is alleged that the child is or may be a child of the family.

If the court is not satisfied with any of these matters then it may require you to file an affidavit verifying what you have stated, and may make such order as it thinks fit. Again, you may need to seek legal advice if this is the case.

If you are the respondent and the petitioner does not apply for the decree absolute, then you may yourself apply after three months from the earliest date when the petitioner could have applied (that is, six weeks plus three months from the date of the decree nisi). Note, however, that such an application cannot simply be dealt with through the post, as can an application by the petitioner – a hearing would be fixed for the court to consider the application. Once again, in this instance you should seek legal advice.

Lastly, note that if the divorce is proceeding on the respondent's cross-petition (see below) then, when it comes to the application for decree absolute, they are in the position of the petitioner so far as everything I have said above, and the petitioner is in the position of the respondent. Accordingly, the respondent could then apply for the decree absolute six weeks after the decree nisi, and the petitioner would have to wait another three months.

AMENDED AND SUPPLEMENTAL PETITIONS

Sometimes it is necessary to amend the divorce petition. This can be for one of two reasons: you may want to correct an error in the petition (or may be required to do so by the court – see also what I said above regarding question 2 of the affidavit in support of the petition) or you may want to add to the allegations (or particulars) in the petition. If the latter, then you can amend the petition if the further particulars alleged occurred before the date of the petition, but if they occurred after that date then you will need to file a supplemental petition. Note that a supplemental petition is not another petition, but merely supplements the original petition. Accordingly, you could not use a supplemental petition to add an allegation of separation to the petition if the requisite period of separation were not complete at the date of the petition – the same thing applies to amending a petition.

An amended or supplemental petition may be filed without the court's permission (or leave) at any time before the respondent has filed an answer to the petition, but may only be filed with the court's leave once an answer has been filed.

Generally speaking, if you wish (or are required) to amend a petition or file a supplementary petition you would be best advised to see a solicitor. Accordingly, the procedure is not explained here. However, if all that is required is a simple amendment of a minor error, then all that is required is to make the amendments in red and file two copies of the amended petition with the court, along with the £80 fee. The court will then send one copy to the respondent, along with a fresh acknowledgement of service form for them to complete.

DEFENDED DIVORCE AND CROSS PETITIONS

Defended divorce is really beyond the scope of this book and is one of those occasions when you would probably need to instruct a solicitor. However, defended divorces are extremely rare and defending a divorce petition is usually no more than a delaying tactic by the respondent, in the hope that the petitioner will reconsider and perhaps agree a reconciliation. Be aware that it is extremely unlikely that you will be able to successfully defend a divorce, defending will substantially add to the costs and you run the risk of being ordered to pay the petitioner's costs, in addition to your own.

Cross petitions are rather more common. What the respondent is saying here is that the breakdown of the marriage was not their fault, but the fault of the petitioner. For example, in a cross petition the respondent may deny that they have behaved unreasonably and allege that the marriage broke down as a result of the petitioner's unreasonable behaviour. My advice here is to try to come to an agreement as to who divorces who, rather than go to the expense of asking the court to decide the matter. You can then ask the court to allow the divorce to proceed either on the original petition or on the cross petition. Hopefully, such matters will have been agreed before the divorce proceedings were issued (see above).

If you do wish to defend the divorce then, in addition to filing your acknowledgement of service, you will have to file an answer to the petition, usually within 28 days of receiving the petition. The answer will usually contain your detailed responses to the allegations made against you in the petition, but may contain a simple denial of allegations. An example of a simple denial of allegations answer and cross petition can be found in Appendix 1. You will need to file the answer or answer and cross petition with the court, together with a copy for the petitioner and the court fee of £200.

Once the divorce is defended, the procedure thereafter is completely different from the procedure in an undefended divorce, unless it subsequently becomes undefended. One of the parties will have to apply to the court for a hearing to be fixed, at which the court will give directions as to how the matter is to proceed and fix a date for the final, contested hearing, when the court will decide whether to grant the divorce (likely), to whom, and who should pay the costs, which will be substantial. Such hearings are, however, extremely unusual nowadays, as the vast majority of divorces are undefended.

2

Children

Agree Arrangements if You Can!

This cannot be stressed enough. Contested applications to the court relating to arrangements for children are the most stressful thing that can happen in a divorce for all concerned, including the children. Unless such an application is made (or unless the court is not satisfied with arrangements), the law takes a 'hands off' approach and leaves the arrangements to the parents to sort out. Accordingly, if arrangements can be agreed between the parents then the court will usually make no order relating to the children.

If you cannot agree arrangements for the children directly with your spouse then consider going to mediation – see Chapter 6.

Residence and Shared Residence

In my view, the starting-point for any negotiations over arrangements for children should be shared residence, although this is not (as yet) stated in the law. As a matter of law, the term 'shared residence' does not necessarily mean the children spending equal amounts of time with each parent, but this is what I am suggesting, at least as a starting-point. From that starting-point the parents should then look at practicalities, such as whether each parent has (or can obtain) suitable accommodation for the children and whether each party's work commitments have any bearing upon their ability to look after the children (it may be possible to alter work commitments but it is obviously not usually practical for either party to give up full-time work – certainly, a court would usually be against this). For other possible factors, see the section below setting out the principles involved in deciding disputes relating to children. Hopefully, once all relevant factors have been considered, the parents will then come to an agreement as to how the children will share their time between them after the separation. As mentioned above, if such an agreement is reached then no court order will usually be made.

If no agreement can be reached, then either parent may apply to the court for a residence order. Note that 'residence' means only that – save for being able to take the child abroad for less than one month without requiring the written consent of the other parent or a court order, the parent with a residence order has no greater rights over the child than the other parent. 'Parental responsibility' (essentially the right to have a say in major decisions relating to the child's upbringing) is still shared by the parents. (Married parents will both have parental responsibility automatically.) Note also that there is no longer any such thing as a custody order, although the term 'custody' is still in common usage.

If an application for a residence order is made, then the court is likely to do one of three things:

1   Make a sole residence order in favour of one of the parents, meaning that the child/children spend most of their time with that parent; or

2   Make a shared residence order which will not necessarily mean that the child/children share their time equally with each parent (see above).

3   Make no order at all, usually where the parents have settled the matter by agreement.

CONTACT

Where it has been established (by agreement or order) that the children will spend most of their time with one parent, arrangements will then have to be made for the other parent's contact with the children. 'Contact ' essentially means the same as the old term 'access', and can include indirect contact, such as telephone contact and contact by letter or email. There are no hard and fast rules about contact and the amount of contact depends upon many factors (see below), but typical contact for all but the youngest children might be every other weekend, one evening a week and half of all school holidays.

If contact cannot be agreed between the parents then one of them may apply to the court for a contact order. A contact order is an order requiring the person with whom a child lives, or is to live, to allow the child to visit or to stay with the person named in the order, or to allow such other contact between the child and that person (for example, telephone contact) as the court specifies. The order will define when, where and how the contact is to take place, for example that contact shall take place every Sunday from 10am to 5pm, with the father collecting the child from, and returning him to, the mother's home. This has the benefit of certainty but of course has the drawback of inflexibility – for example, when one parent cannot keep to the arrangement due to work or other commitments. It is very difficult to incorporate flexibility into a contact order and this is another reason why arrangements should be agreed if possible.

The contact order may also include conditions, such as that the contact take place at a specific location or under the supervision of a specific person.

On an application for a contact order, the court may do one of the following:

- Make an order setting out the contact arrangements (which may or may not be the arrangements the parties are seeking); or

- Before making a contact order, make a contact activity direction requiring a party to the proceedings to take part in an activity that promotes contact with the child concerned, for example programmes, classes and counselling or guidance sessions to assist a person 'as regards establishing, maintaining or improving contact with a child', or addressing a person's violent behaviour to 'enable or facilitate contact with a child', or 'sessions in which information or advice is given as regards making or operating arrangements for contact with a child, including making arrangements by means of mediation'; or

- It may (unusually) refuse to make an order if it considers that no contact is appropriate; or

- It may make no order if matters are agreed and it is considered that no order is needed.

OTHER ORDERS

In addition to residence and contact orders, the court can also make prohibited steps orders and specific issue orders.

A prohibited steps order is defined as 'an order that no step which could be taken by a parent in meeting his parental responsibility for a child, and which is of a kind specified in the order, shall be taken by any person without the consent of the court'. A typical example is an order prohibiting a parent from taking any step that may result in the child being known by a new name.

A specific issue order is defined as 'an order giving directions for the purpose of determining a specific question which has arisen, or which may arise, in connection with any aspect of parental responsibility for a child'. An example of such an issue is a dispute between the parents over their child's schooling – the court will decide which school the child should attend.

PRINCIPLES INVOLVED IN DECIDING DISPUTES

In determining any question relating to the upbringing of a child, the child's welfare is the court's paramount consideration. Known as the 'paramountcy principle', this is always the overriding factor.

In deciding whether to make an order relating to a child the court will have regard to all of the circumstances and in particular the following:

■ **The ascertainable wishes and feelings of the child concerned (considered in the light of his or her age and understanding).** There are no hard and fast age rules relating to this, but a reasonable rule of thumb might be that the court would pay some attention to the wishes of a child under 10, considerable attention to the wishes of a child between 10 and 14, and would be likely to follow the wishes of a child over 14, unless they were clearly unreasonable. Obviously, the court will be alert to the possibility of one parent trying to turn the child against the other but this can still cause great problems, especially with older children where it may be impossible to force them to do something against their wishes.

- **His or her physical, emotional and educational needs.** This can cover such things as physical disability, long-term illness, special health needs and special educational needs. Obviously, these matters can have a significant bearing upon the child's welfare. It also covers basic matters such as housing, including suitable sleeping arrangements for the child.

- **The likely effect on him/her of any change in his/her circumstances.** This can be relevant to contact applications but is most relevant to applications involving a change of residence, especially where there is considerable distance between the homes of the parents. Such matters as change of schools and moving away from friends can be particularly relevant. There is also the issue of changing long-standing arrangements, which may have a disturbing effect upon the child.

- **His/her age, sex, background and any characteristics of his/ hers which the court considers relevant.** This is less often a factor than most of the other circumstances listed here. It is sometimes argued that young children and teenage girls are better off residing with their mothers, although such arguments carry less weight now than they used to do.

More relevant, perhaps, is the situation where the child has a particular emotional attachment to one parent.

■ **Any harm which he or she has suffered or is at risk of suffering.** This can include emotional as well as physical harm. Obviously, if the child has suffered harm previously whilst in the care of one parent, whether by that parent's actions or neglect, then this will be a very important factor in any application. There may also be concerns about the level of care which one parent can give in the future, which often links with the final matter:

■ **How capable each of his or her parents, and any other person in relation to whom the court considers the question to be relevant, is of meeting his or her needs.** This, of course, relates primarily to parenting skills. Again, the age of the child can be a factor, with mothers of young children arguing that only they have the necessary skills to look after the child. Also relevant though are the practicalities such as work commitments – if these necessitate the child being left with a carer or relative, then their capability of meeting the child's needs also becomes relevant.

APPLICATIONS TO THE COURT

The procedure is that one party makes the application and the court will fix an initial directions appointment to which both parties must attend. The directions appointment is usually in two parts. Firstly, the parties (usually without their lawyers) will have a meeting with a Children and Family Court Advisory and Support Service (Cafcass) officer, at which the officer will ascertain the issues involved and investigate the possibility of the matter being resolved by agreement, possibly with the assistance of mediation. At the end of the meeting, the Cafcass officer will prepare a short note of the outcome, which will be passed to the district judge. The parties and their lawyers will then be called before the district judge. If an agreement has been reached, then the court may make a contact order in those terms if it thinks that an order is required, for example to ensure that the parties keep to the agreed arrangements. If there is a partial agreement for some limited contact to take place, the court may adjourn the case for, say, three months to see how that contact proceeds, and then fix another directions hearing to review the matter. If no agreement is reached but the parties agree to go to mediation, then the court may adjourn the case for a period to allow the mediation to take place. If no agreement at all is reached, then the court will give directions as to how the matter is to proceed. These directions may include the filing of written statements by the parties and any witnesses, the preparation of a welfare report if appropriate and the fixing of a final hearing date (although in practice the final hearing date is not usually fixed until later). These matters will be dealt with in further detail below.

An application for a residence order, contact order, prohibited steps order or specific issue order is made on form C100, which can be found in Appendix 1 under Example Children Application. As will be seen, most of the form is reasonably straightforward to complete and there is a very helpful guidance booklet (CB1) available. However, the following sections need some explanation:

Summary of application: Tick the box 'Permission not required'. The respondent is, of course, the other parent (who may, confusingly, be the petitioner in the divorce).

Section 1: You must give your address to the court but may not wish to give it to the respondent. As the respondent will be served with a copy of the form, you will need to complete a confidential address form C8, if you wish to omit your address from the C100 form. You will normally be the only applicant, so the 'Applicant 2' section can be ignored.

Section 3: Set out *briefly* what order you are seeking and why. You do *not* need to go into any great detail (you will have a opportunity to file a detailed written statement, if necessary – see below) and you should keep what you say *relevant* to the issue. For example, on a contact application a simple 'My wife won't let me see the children so I am seeking a contact order ' will be sufficient.

Section 4: *Parenting Plan* is a booklet prepared by the Department for Education and Skills giving information to separating parents. It can be obtained from the court office, Citizens Advice Bureau or, in PDF form, from the Cafcass website – see Appendix 2. You can use the advice in the booklet to draw up an agreed plan for your children, although obviously if you are now making an application to the court this will be unlikely, unless the plan has broken down. If this is the case you should attach a copy of the plan to the form and explain why the plan has broken down. You will also need to state whether you have used mediation – see Chapter 6.

Section 5: As stated on the form, if you answer 'Yes' to this question, then you will also need to complete a supplemental information form C1A, giving further details of the alleged abuse, violence or harm. You can obtain this form from the court office. Note that if there are allegations of abuse, violence or harm, then the court will usually deal with these as a separate preliminary issue at a fact-finding hearing, where it will decide upon the truth of the allegations.

Section 8: This relates to other interested parties, such as anyone else who is caring for the child, other than the parents. The section can therefore usually be left blank.

Once you have completed the form, you should send it to the court, together with a copy for the respondent, two copies of any form C1A and the court fee of £175. The court will then fix a date for the initial directions hearing and send you a notice of proceedings form (C6) with the hearing date on it, a sealed copy of the C100 form and an acknowledgement form (C7). You will have to send all of these to the respondent (keeping copies for yourself) and file a statement of service form (which the court should also have sent to you) with the court, confirming which documents you have sent to the respondent, and when, where and how you sent them.

The acknowledgement is a simple form, which the respondent should complete, stating whether or not they oppose the making of the order that the applicant is seeking. Copies of the acknowledgement should be filed with the court and served on the applicant within 14 days of the respondent receiving the application.

As mentioned above, if no agreement can be reached at the initial hearing, then the court will give directions as to what should be done next and how the matter should proceed. These can deal with any relevant issues but the most common directions are for the filing of written statements and the preparation of a welfare report.

If the filing of written statements is ordered, the court will direct that each party and their witnesses file them with the court and serve copies on the other party by a set date. There is no set form for a statement but I suggest that the parties' own statements be set out in numbered paragraphs starting with a brief history of the matter, going through the six factors set out above under 'Principles involved in deciding disputes', and concluding with a paragraph setting out exactly what order or orders they are asking the court to make. All statements should:

1   be dated;

2   be signed by the person making the statement;

3   contain a declaration that the maker of the statement believes it to be true and understands that it may be placed before the court; and

4   show in the top right hand corner of the first page –

   a)   the initials and surname of the person making the statement,

   b)   the number of the statement in relation to the maker (i.e. that it is their first or second statement etc.),

   c)   the date on which the statement was made, and

   d)   the party on whose behalf it is filed.

You can also attach relevant documents, such as copies of school reports, to the statement.

So far as witnesses are concerned, these may, for example, be other family members or close friends, but make sure that they have something relevant to say and are not just repeating what you have already said. Also make sure that they are aware that they will have to attend any final hearing to give evidence in court and, possibly, be cross-examined by the other party's lawyer.

Once the statements have been signed, they should be filed with the court and copies should be sent to the other party *and* to the Cafcass officer if a welfare report has been ordered.

The court will direct that a welfare report be prepared, normally by a Cafcass officer, if it considers this to be necessary, which it usually does in all but the most straightforward cases. Note that this could entail substantial delay – in some areas of the country it can take more than six months for the report to be prepared. This can cause considerable hardship, especially if you are seeking a contact order and the other party is denying contact – in this case you should consider asking the court to make an interim contact order, which would at least give you some limited contact, until the matter is finally determined. The Cafcass officer may also try to arrange some contact, as part of their work in preparing the report.

The Cafcass officer essentially has a free hand as to how he or she should conduct their enquiries prior to the preparation of their report, but these normally include interviewing the parties, seeing the children with the parties and making other relevant enquiries, for example with the child's school. It is *essential* that you cooperate fully with the Cafcass officer, as their report will normally conclude with a recommendation as to what order or orders the court should make and it is highly likely that the court will follow that recommendation. In fact, if the matter has not already been settled with the assistance of the Cafcass officer, it often is settled once the report is prepared, as it is then usually very clear what order the court is likely to make at a final, contested hearing.

If the recommendation of the Cafcass officer is substantially different from what you are seeking and you still wish to proceed to a contested hearing, then you will need to instruct a lawyer to represent you, if you have not done so already, as you will need to ask the court to direct that the Cafcass officer attend the hearing to be cross-examined, and this is a job for a lawyer. Even if the recommendation is in your favour and it is the other party who wishes to proceed with a contested hearing, I would still advise that you instruct a lawyer to represent you.

ENFORCING AND VARYING ORDERS

Once you have got your order, agreed or otherwise, that unfortunately is not always the end of the matter, as orders are often breached, especially contact orders. Again, this subject is really beyond the scope of this book, but a couple of general points follow.

The first thing to be aware of is that a court order relating to arrangements for children is not 'written in stone' in the same way as other types of court order. You can't just go back to the court six months or a year after the order was made and expect the court to enforce it without looking into the matter afresh. Things can change and what was best for the child's welfare when the order was made is not necessarily still best for the child. So, for example, instead of enforcing a contact order the court may instead redefine the contact arrangements to deal with any problems that have arisen since the original order was made. Enforcement action is unlikely unless there is a blatant and inexcusable breach of the order; even more likely if there has been a series of such breaches.

If the court does take enforcement action then these are the options open to it:

■ Impose a fine upon the person in breach of the order, although this will of course only be appropriate if that person has the means to pay.

■ Commit the person in breach of the order to prison, but this may not be practically possible if they are the parent looking after the child, although in an extreme case the court can order that the child reside with the other parent (if that parent is in a position to look after the child).

■ On the application of the other party (form C79), make an order (an enforcement order) imposing an unpaid work requirement on the person in breach of the contact order, provided that the contact order contains a notice warning of the consequences of failing to comply with it. All contact orders made on or after 8 December 2008 should contain such a notice and either party can apply to the court (form C78) for such a notice to be attached to contact orders made before that date.

■ On the application of the other party (again, form C79), make an order that the person in breach of the contact order pay financial compensation to the other party for any losses that they incurred as a result of the failure to comply with the contact order. Again, the requirement of a warning notice applies, as above.

Residence and contact orders can be varied at any time by the agreement of the parents and will automatically cease to have effect if the parents should subsequently live together for a continuous period of more than six months. On the other hand, you may wish to change the arrangements but the other parent may not agree, for example where you now seek more contact than was contained in the original order. In this case you can apply back to the court for the order to be varied. Note, however, that you will need to give the original order some time to work (say, at least six months) and you cannot make continual applications to the court, as the court can make an order forbidding any further applications without the permission of the court.

3

Child Maintenance

AGREE IF YOU CAN!

Even if the parent with care ('PWC' – the parent with whom the children spend most of their time) is in receipt of state benefits, then it is not obligatory to make an application to the Child Support Agency (CSA). In other words, the law leaves it to parents to agree the amount of child maintenance if they can. Only if they cannot agree will one or other of them (obviously normally the PWC) make an application to the Agency. Note that courts cannot make child maintenance orders, save in the limited circumstances mentioned below.

If the Agency is not being used, there is no obligation to use the child support formula (see below) but obviously it is a useful guidance in most cases, save where the non-resident parent ('NRP' – the parent with whom the children spend less time) has a particularly high income. In such a case, I would suggest that they should pay more than the formula would require them to pay – a figure that has some relation to the standard of living enjoyed by the parents prior to the separation.

If an agreement is reached, the parents can draw up a written private agreement form, an example of which can be found on the Child Maintenance Options website – see Appendix 2. Note, however, that such an agreement is not enforceable – if one parent fails to keep to the agreement, then the other will need to apply to the CSA.

HOW MUCH? – THE CHILD SUPPORT FORMULA

In essence, the child support formula is simple: the NRP pays 15% of their net income for one child, 20% for two children and 25% for three or more children. This is known as the basic rate. 'Net income' essentially means gross income less income tax, national insurance and pension contributions (75% of pension contributions if the pension is set up to pay off a mortgage). Note that the NRP pays less if their net weekly income is less than £200. If their income is more than £100 per week but less than £200 per week, they will pay the reduced rate of £5 plus 25% of their weekly income over £100 for one child, £5 plus 35% of their weekly income over £100 for two children and £5 plus 45% of their weekly income over £100 for three or more children. If the NRP's net weekly income is between £5 and £100 per week (or they or their partner receive income support or certain other state benefits) they pay the flat rate of £5, and if their income is less than £5 a week they pay nothing – the nil rate.

Example 1: Three children, NRP's net weekly income = £300, NRP pays 25% of £300 = £75

Example 2: One child, NRP's net weekly income = £160, NRP pays £5 plus 25% of £60 (£15) = £20

Where the child stays overnight with the NRP one night a week on average, maintenance will be reduced by one seventh, two sevenths for two nights per week and three sevenths for three nights per week. If care is shared equally, then it is reduced by half plus £7, although I would suggest that a fairer arrangement would be to take into account the net income of each parent. If each has a similar income, then neither should pay anything; if one has a higher income, then they should make a contribution to the other parent, which can hopefully be agreed.

Example 3: Two children, stay with NRP 104 nights per year. NRP's net weekly income = £350. NRP pays 20% of £350 = £70, reduced by 2/7 = £50

If the NRP has other children living with them and the basic rate applies, their net weekly income for the purpose of calculating child maintenance will be reduced by 15% for one child, 20% for two children and 25% for three or more children. If the NRP pays the reduced rate, then the percentages referred to above are reduced, in accordance with Table 3.1.

Example 4: Two children, NRP has one child living with them, NRP's net weekly income = £300. NRP's income reduced by 15% to £255. NRP pays 20% of £255 = £51

If the NRP has to pay child maintenance to more than one PWC (for example, a father who has children by two different mothers), then the total child maintenance is calculated as above and then divided equally between each of the children.

Number of children needing child maintenance	Number of children living with the non-resident parent	Standard amount	Percentage of net weekly income over £100 a week, but less than £200, that a non-resident parent pays
1	1	£5	20.5%
	2	£5	19%
	3 or more	£5	17.5%
2	1	£5	29%
	2	£5	27%
	3 or more	£5	25%
3 or more	1	£5	37.5%
	2	£5	35%
	3 or more	£5	32.5%

Table 3.1   Reduced rates for NRPs with other children

A child maintenance calculator can be found on the CSA's website:

https:/secureonline.dwp.gov.uk/csa/v2/en/calculate-maintenance.asp.

Note that the CSA is being replaced by the Child Maintenance and Enforcement Commission (see Appendix 2) and the Commission will use a new formula, based upon gross rather than net income. At the time of writing, it is expected that the new formula will come into operation during 2011.

HOW LONG? – DURATION OF PAYMENTS

This is a matter open to agreement but if no agreement is reached then the duration of child maintenance payments will depend upon whether the payments are made through the CSA. If they are, the maintenance will last until the child reaches the age of 16, or if they are still in full-time education, until they reach the age of 19. If the payments are made in accordance with a court order then their duration will depend upon the terms of the order.

A typical court order may specify that the maintenance shall continue until the child reaches the age of 18 years or ceases full-time secondary (or tertiary) education, whichever shall be the later.

AGREED COURT ORDERS

The most common instance in which the court can still make a child maintenance order is where the maintenance is agreed as part of a divorce settlement. However, after 12 months have elapsed from the date of the order, either party may then apply to the CSA for a child support assessment, which may obviously be for a different amount to the order, and the assessment will replace the order.

APPLYING FOR CHILD SUPPORT

An application for child support can be made online via the CSA's website (www.csa.gov.uk), by telephone to the appropriate child support office for your area or by completing a form (either by hand after printing it from the website or online and then printing off). The application requires you to give details about yourself, details about the children and details about the other parent, so far as they are known to you.

Once the application has been made the Agency will contact the NRP, usually by phone, to gather the information it requires to make an assessment. The Agency says that it aims to make the assessment within 12 weeks of the application but admits that it can take up to six months.

DEALING WITH THE CHILD SUPPORT AGENCY

Dealing with the CSA can be an extremely frustrating process, both for the PWC and the NRP. The best advice that I can give is that you should be persistent, but don't make a nuisance of yourself. If you think the Agency is not dealing with something as quickly as it should, then chase them. On the other hand, give them a reasonable time to deal with matters, as unnecessary chasing is only going to slow the process down, not just for you but also for other users.

If you are the PWC, then give the Agency as many details as you can about the NRP, their whereabouts and their means. If you believe that they have failed to disclose all of their income, then give details of their lifestyle, if you feel it is inconsistent with the income disclosed. Don't forget to give any details you have of the NRP's capital assets (apart from their home), as these may increase the amount of child support if the assets are worth more than £65,000.

If you are the NRP then you should respond quickly to, and cooperate with, the Agency. If you fail to cooperate, the Agency may make a 'default maintenance decision' whereby the Agency requires you to pay £30 a week for one child, £40 a week for two children and £50 a week for three or more children, until they get the information they require from you to make a maintenance calculation. If the calculation arrives at a lower figure than the default maintenance decision, you will still be liable for the default figure until the date of the calculation (if the calculation arrives at a higher figure, then you will have to make up the difference from the date the default maintenance decision started).

The NRP should also inform the Agency of any relevant special expenses, which may reduce the amount they are required to pay. These include costs relating to your contact with the children and the cost of paying certain debts incurred when you and the PWC lived together.

ENFORCING PAYMENT

As the court can only make agreed child maintenance orders, it is extremely rare that it is necessary to enforce a child maintenance order, so the following only deals with enforcement of child support.

The CSA has two courses open to it to enforce payment of child support:

- If the NRP is an employee, it can take money direct from their earnings (a 'deduction from earnings order'); or

- It can take action through the courts.

A deduction from earnings order can be made when the NRP works for an employer or receives an occupational pension. This is normally the first method of enforcement where the NRP is employed. The CSA tells the employer how much to deduct and the employer must pass that sum on to the CSA. The employer can also take up to £1 for their administrative costs. Note that if the NRP changes employer or becomes unemployed, they must notify the CSA. Note also that if the deduction by the employer is insufficient to pay the child support, then the CSA may also take the NRP to court to recover the balance.

If the CSA takes action through the courts, then the first step will be to apply to a magistrates' court for a liability order, which enables the CSA to take further action to recover payment of child support. Obtaining a liability order is virtually a formality – the court can't question the maintenance assessment and must make the order if the NRP is in arrears with payments of child support. Once the liability order has been made, the CSA can take the following action:

- Instruct bailiffs to seize the NRP's belongings and sell them to raise the money to pay the amount owed; or

- Have the order entered on the Register of Judgments, Orders and Fines, which will affect the NRP's credit rating; or

- Apply to a County Court for a third party debt order, requiring a third party such as the NRP's bank to freeze money in the NRP's account and pay it to the CSA, or for a charging order against any property owned by the NRP, attaching the debt to that property (and if necessary requiring the property to be sold so that the debt is paid); or

■ Apply to a magistrates' court for the NRP to be disqualified from driving or to be committed to prison for up to six weeks.

Note that the Child Maintenance and Enforcement Commission (see above) will have new enforcement powers from 2009/10, including the power to take money from bank accounts itself.

WHEN THE CSA CANNOT DEAL WITH THE MATTER

The CSA does not have jurisdiction to make a child support maintenance assessment in the following circumstances:

■ Where the payer is not the natural or adoptive parent (the court can order such a person to pay child maintenance where they were married to a parent and they treated the child as a child of the family); or

■ Where one of the parents or the child is not habitually resident in the UK; or

■ Where the parents have not separated.

In such a case, an application for child maintenance may be made to a court.

SCHOOL FEES AND TOP-UP ORDERS

The duty to maintain a child includes a duty to cause the child to be educated, therefore school fees are part of a child's maintenance. However, the amount of child support/maintenance may obviously be insufficient to cover the fees. It may therefore be necessary for the parents to reach agreement on who should pay the school fees, separately from child support/maintenance. Any such agreement can be included in a separation agreement or consent order. Note, however, that an order that includes a provision for one parent to contribute towards school fees can prevent the other parent from subsequently making an application to the Child Support Agency.

Lastly, if the NRP's net income exceeds £2,000 per week, then only the first £2,000 will be taken into account for the purpose of child support – there is therefore a maximum amount of child support. In these circumstances, the court can make a top-up order, requiring the NRP to pay over and above the maximum amount of child support.

4

Finances and Property

GENERAL PRINCIPLES

Sorting out the financial settlement on divorce is often the biggest battleground, but it does not have to be so. The basic principles are actually quite simple and reaching a financial settlement should be relatively straightforward in the majority of cases, so long as both parties understand those principles.

The starting-point in all cases is equal division of all assets. However, either party can claim that they are entitled to more than 50% of the assets for any relevant reason, the most common of which are needs (that is, their needs are greater than the other party's needs) and contributions (that is, their financial contribution to the marital assets was substantially greater than the other party's contribution). These will be discussed in more detail below.

Establishing the matrimonial assets' value

What, then, are the assets? Unless your financial assets are very few, I recommend that a schedule of assets be drawn up and, if possible, agreed with your spouse. An asset schedule simply lists all of the assets and their values, usually in three columns, one for joint assets and one for assets belonging to each party, totalled at the bottom. Note the following:

1   Written confirmation of asset valuations should be obtained, if possible, such as bank statements, share valuations, endowment policy surrender valuations, and so on.

2   Only include assets of significant value – say, £500. Personal possessions should not be included (they will usually remain the property of that person), unless they are of high value, such as items of jewellery.

3   Similarly, furniture should not be included save for items of high value, such as antiques. Remember that the court values assets *as at the time of the settlement*, so the current, second-hand value is what counts, not the original purchase price. Obviously, the second-hand value of most items of furniture is minimal, so it is generally not worth arguing over division of furniture – even where both parties have solicitors, the solicitors normally leave it to the parties themselves to agree division of furniture.

4   The valuation of the (former) matrimonial home (and any other properties) is often a sticking point. At least one written professional valuation should definitely be obtained – two or more will give a more accurate picture. Most estate agents will offer a free valuation but make sure this is a *market* valuation (that is, how much the property will actually realise on sale) and not just, for example, a valuation for a quick sale. Do *not* rely on mortgage valuations – mortgage companies are only concerned that the value of the property will cover the amount they are lending, not with the full value of the property. The most accurate valuation will come with a full

structural survey, but these are expensive. Once again, the value of the property should be agreed with your spouse. This can be achieved, for example, by each party obtaining their own professional valuation and, if they differ, agreeing a figure mid-way between the two. Alternatively, the parties may agree to jointly instruct one professional valuer (and share the valuer's fees) and agree to be bound by the valuation.

5   Pension valuations must be obtained. The figure that the court will require is the cash equivalent transfer value (CETV), or the amount that could be transferred out of that pension fund into another. Some pension providers include a CETV on the annual statement that they send out to the pension holder, otherwise you will need to request a written CETV from the provider. Note that some CETVs provide a less realistic picture of the real value of the pension than others and can considerably underestimate the real value of the pension. This can be especially true of public sector pension schemes, especially police and army pensions. If in any doubt, you should consult an actuary or at least an independent financial adviser. Once the pension valuation has been obtained and agreed, it can be put in the asset schedule, either with all of the other assets, or separately, if pensions are going to be dealt with by way of pension sharing – see below.

6   It is arguable that certain assets should not be included as matrimonial property. The most common of these is inheritances – the party that received the inheritance arguing that they should keep it, without it being taken into account as part of their share of the matrimonial assets. Note, however, that there is no rule that inheritances should be left out of account. I would suggest that the argument is more likely to

succeed in short marriages or, perhaps, where the inheritance was received shortly before or after the parties separate. In longer marriages the argument is less likely to be successful, especially where the inheritance has been spent. For example, where the inheritance, or part of it, has been spent on the matrimonial home, then it clearly becomes matrimonial property, as the matrimonial home is always a matrimonial asset.

Dividing the matrimonial assets

Having established the value of the matrimonial assets available, the next question is, of course, how should they be divided? Having stated above that the starting-point in all cases is equal division of all assets unless there is a good reason to depart from equality, we need to consider in detail what would constitute a good reason for such a departure. Section 25 of the Matrimonial Causes Act 1973 sets out a (non-exhaustive) list of the factors to which the court should have regard when considering a financial settlement, and these give some clues as to what would constitute a good reason:

a) **The income, earning capacity, property and other financial resources which each of the parties to the marriage has or is likely to have in the foreseeable future, including in the case of earning capacity any increase in that capacity which it would in the opinion of the court be reasonable to expect a party to the marriage to take steps to acquire** – This one is pretty obvious and self-explanatory. If one party's income is substantially greater than the other party's income, then the other party can claim a greater than half share of the assets to compensate, although this is usually argued under needs –

see below. Note that income includes earning capacity, which should be used if one party can or will in the foreseeable future clearly earn more than they are earning at present. As to property, this factor really just deals with the ascertaining of the assets for division, as described above. Note, however, that if one spouse is going to acquire an asset in the foreseeable future, then that could be a good reason for the other spouse to receive more than half of the assets currently available.

b) **The financial needs, obligations and responsibilities which each of the parties to the marriage has or is likely to have in the foreseeable future** – As indicated above, this is one of the most common reasons to depart from equality of division. The most likely reason why one party's needs are greater than the other's is that they will be looking after the children. Specifically, they will need accommodation suitable not just for them but also for the children. For example, if there are two children and they are to reside with the wife then, on the face of it, she could argue that she needs a three-bedroom property, whereas the husband only needs a one-bedroom property. As mentioned above, this can be linked with disparity in incomes so, for example, if the wife has a lower income then her mortgage capacity will be less, and she can therefore argue that she needs a greater share of the capital. Where the matrimonial home has not been sold, needs can also be addressed by allowing the wife to remain in the matrimonial home until the children have grown up. In this case, it will still have to be decided how the net proceeds will be divided after the property is eventually sold. Note that in high-money cases the greater needs of one party may not be relevant, where they can be met by a half share of the matrimonial assets.

c) **The standard of living enjoyed by the family before the breakdown of the marriage** – Again, this is only usually relevant in high-money cases, as in most other cases it is a simple fact of life that when a couple split up each party will have to suffer a lowering in their standard of living.

d) **The age of each party to the marriage and the duration of the marriage** – If one party is significantly older than the other then they could argue that they should have a greater than half share of the assets, as they have less working life left to build up assets. A specific example here would be re-housing – an older person would not be able to borrow so much on mortgage, as the mortgage term would have to be shorter. Also relevant is whether or not one of the parties is at or approaching retirement age, as obviously their income is likely to be less in retirement. As to the duration of the marriage, this does not usually have much effect upon the amount of a settlement unless it is a very short marriage, in which case it can be argued that the parties should just be put back in the same financial position they were each in prior to the marriage. What constitutes a short marriage is not defined, but the courts generally seem to interpret the term quite strictly. Accordingly, a marriage of three years or more is not considered to be short, so a very short marriage is probably one that lasted no more than a year before it broke down. Duration of the marriage can also be relevant to contributions – see below.

e) **Any physical or mental disability of either of the parties to the marriage** – Pretty obvious and again part of the needs argument, for example, a disabled party might need extra money to convert their home to meet the needs of their disability. Note, however, that a terminal illness could actually *reduce* needs, especially if life expectancy is very short – that party only needs to provide for themself for a short period of time and the court would not be concerned about providing for the beneficiaries of their estate.

f) **The contributions which each of the parties has made or is likely in the foreseeable future to make to the welfare of the family, including any contribution by looking after the home or caring for the family** – A common argument, especially by husbands, is that they were the main or only breadwinner during the marriage and that therefore they should have the lion's share of the assets. As this factor makes clear, this is not true. It is more accurate to consider that his contribution is equalled by the wife's contribution, in looking after the home and bringing up the family. In most cases, contributions are made at the outset of the marriage, for example one party putting in significantly more money to the purchase of the matrimonial home. That party will seek to recover those contributions by claiming a greater than half share of the matrimonial assets. Here, the duration of the marriage can be relevant, as the longer it goes on the weaker the argument usually becomes – the assets become 'mixed' over time and can no longer be said to belong to one party or the other. If a financial contribution is made later in the marriage (not including an inheritance – see above), this generally can only be recovered if the total assets are enough so that the other party is left with sufficient to meet their needs.

g) **The conduct of each of the parties, if that conduct is such that it would in the opinion of the court be inequitable to disregard it** – It is often argued that the other party should receive less due to their conduct but it is very rare that this is actually relevant to the financial settlement. Certainly, adultery and most forms of unreasonable behaviour will have no bearing. To be relevant the conduct will have to be of a very serious nature, such as a threat to kill, and even then this is no guarantee that a court would penalise that party by reducing the amount of their settlement. Note that conduct during the course of the proceedings, such as failing to cooperate or comply with the requirements of the court, is not usually penalised by a lower settlement but can be penalised by an order that that party pay a contribution towards the other party's costs.

h) **The value to each of the parties to the marriage of any benefit which, by reason of the dissolution or annulment of the marriage, that party will lose the chance of acquiring** – This factor is primarily concerned with pensions. If your spouse has a pension, then you will almost certainly be a potential beneficiary under the pension scheme if they were to die and therefore you will lose that potential benefit when the marriage is dissolved. The ways of dealing with pensions are discussed in more detail below, but could be a reason to depart from an equal division of other assets where one party keeps their pension and the other party has more than half of the other assets to compensate.

Where does all of this leave us? In short, if everything is approximately equal between the parties, including income, capital assets, pensions, needs and contributions then an equal division is appropriate. If not, then an unequal division may be appropriate.

Unequal division of assets

The next question is – if an unequal division is appropriate, then how much should each party receive? This depends upon the reason for the unequal division. If, for example, the reason is that one party contributed more, then it may just be a simple matter of that party receiving that sum back and the rest of the assets being divided equally. Things can, however, get more complicated when the reason is that one party's needs are greater than the others (often linked with that party having a lower income). Here, there is no formula used to calculate each party's share and it is more a case of coming up with a percentage figure (of the total assets) and deciding whether that appears to be fair, after considering how it will leave each party. If, for example, the disparity in needs is relatively small then a 55/45 or a 60/40 division in favour of the party with greater needs may be appropriate. If, on the other hand, the disparity is considerable, then a 70/30 or even an 80/20 division may be appropriate. In extreme cases, it may even be appropriate for one party to receive 100%. An example of this could be where the only asset is the matrimonial home, the wife has a very low income and the husband has a substantial income – the husband might agree to transfer his interest in the property to the wife, in return for the wife making no claim against him for maintenance.

It would be impossible to give examples of all possible scenarios but the following illustrations may assist in showing how settlements are worked out in practice. (Note that each illustration is simplified, both in its facts and its outcome, and assumes that there are no other factors which may influence the settlement. Note also that these are only possible reasonable outcomes – there is no such thing as a 'definitive' outcome to a given set of facts.)

Illustration 1 – Five-year marriage, no children, parties have similar income and needs: simple equal division of capital assets.

Illustration 2 – One-year marriage, no children, parties have similar income and needs but one party made a substantial contribution towards the purchase of the matrimonial home : each party is returned to the financial position they were in prior to the marriage (a factor which could influence this would be if the other party gave up secure accommodation, for example a council house, to move into the matrimonial home).

Illustration 3 – Fifteen-year marriage, two minor children living with the wife, wife on low income, husband earning £30,000 per annum, only asset the matrimonial home, which has an equity of £100,000: wife needs to remain in the home with the children (assuming she can afford to do so), as there are no equally suitable options for the accommodation of herself and the children. Accordingly, the property is not to be sold until the children finish their education, the wife remarries or cohabits (usually for a minimum of six months, to ensure that her new relationship is permanent), whichever shall occur first. Upon sale, the net proceeds are to be divided as to 75% to the wife and 25% to the husband, in view of the wife's greater need for capital to re-house herself due to her lower income.

Illustration 4 – Twenty-year marriage, children grown up, net capital assets £300,000, wife earns £20,000 per annum, husband earns £40,000 per annum: wife agrees to settlement whereby she receives £200,000 in return for a 'clean break' (see below), i.e. no maintenance for herself.

Illustration 5 – Twenty-five-year marriage, children grown up, only asset is matrimonial home (free of mortgage), wife unable to work due to disability, husband earning £50,000 per annum and living with new partner: husband transfers his entire interest to the wife, for no consideration.

Illustration 6 – Ten-year marriage, no children, no capital assets, wife unemployed and husband earning £50,000 per annum: husband pays £1,000 per month maintenance to the wife for a period of two years to enable her to re-gain her financial independence, thereafter there is a clean break.

Illustration 7 – Assets £500,000, husband contributed £100,000, wife's needs assessed at £200,000: husband gets his £100,000 back and the balance of the assets are divided equally, so husband gets £300,000 and wife gets £200,000.

Illustration 8 – Assets £500,000, husband contributed £100,000, wife's needs assessed at £250,000: assets are divided equally, so each party gets £250,000. (Note how needs take precedence over contributions.)

SEPARATING FINANCES AND OTHER PRACTICAL STEPS

The first and most obvious piece of advice is to close any joint accounts to prevent the other party from withdrawing all funds in the account or, worse still, from running up an overdraft, for which you will be jointly liable. Hopefully, the accounts can be closed by agreement, with the parties agreeing the division of any funds in the account. If agreement cannot be reached, you will need to get in touch with the bank. Most banks will not close joint accounts without the agreement of both parties but they will usually freeze the account, thereby preventing any further withdrawals.

Other jointly owned assets will also need to be dealt with, such as joint life policies. You will need to work out whether the policy will be kept and, if so, who will pay the premiums. The policy may be transferred (assigned) into the sole name of one party or it may be cashed in and the proceeds divided between the parties. There are two ways of cashing in an endowment policy: surrendering it to the insurance company (provided the policy has been running for long enough to have acquired a surrender value) or selling it to a company that buys endowment policies. Not all policies can be sold, but if they can they will usually realise more than surrendering the policy – shop around for the best deal.

Similarly, joint debts will need to be dealt with, although here there is much less room for manoeuvre, as creditors will not normally be prepared to release one of two joint debtors. You will therefore need to agree who will be responsible for the debt and ensure that the other party cannot increase it without your consent. If the debt was incurred primarily for joint purposes, it will be treated as a debt of the marriage and taken into account in any financial settlement.

If you vacate the matrimonial home on a permanent basis, then you can have all bills relating to the property transferred to the party remaining in the property, unless you agree to continue paying, or contributing towards, the bills. Although, even where you are contributing it is still advisable to transfer the bill to prevent yourself from being liable for the full amount if the other party doesn't pay. The bills to transfer will include council tax, gas, electricity and telephone. It is not usually necessary to obtain the agreement of the party remaining in the property – just inform the local authority or utility company that you have vacated the property and they should transfer the bill to the other party.

If the matrimonial home is in joint names, then it is most likely owned by you and your spouse as joint tenants, in equal shares. This means that if either of you were to die then the ownership of the whole property will pass automatically to the survivor. Obviously, you may wish to change this. You can do so simply by serving a notice of severance on the other party. You do not need the agreement of the other party, or even an acknowledgement by them that they have received the notice, although you should request the Land Registry to record the change in the way the property is owned. The effect of the notice is to change the ownership to tenants in common, which means that if either party were to die then that party's share in the property would pass into his or her estate and be dealt with under the terms of their Will. Obviously, therefore, you should also make a Will, or a new Will, when you serve the notice to ensure (so far as possible) that your share goes to whoever you want it to go to (if you do not make a Will then your share would probably still go to your spouse under the laws of intestacy, until such time as the marriage is dissolved). Note that severing the joint tenancy does not alter the size of each party's share in the property (that remains to be agreed or determined by the court) and that therefore the court could make an order that frustrates your intentions regarding your share. Note also that severing the joint tenancy can be a double-edged sword, as your spouse may die before the marriage is dissolved and you would not then automatically acquire their share in the property.

If the matrimonial home is owned solely by your spouse then you should register your right to occupy the property at the Land Registry. This will prevent your spouse from selling or mortgaging the property without reference to you. Registering a home rights notice is a simple procedure – you just have to complete form HR1 (available on the Land Registry's website, www.landregistry.gov.uk) and send it to your local Land Registry. There is no fee to pay but note that the Land Registry will inform your spouse that the notice has been registered. Note also that the notice expires when the divorce is finalised – it is therefore essential, where the property is owned by your spouse, to resolve the issue of your interest in the property before the divorce is finalised.

So far as the contents of the matrimonial home are concerned, my advice is to agree their division if at all possible. Unless you own antique furniture or other items of value such as paintings, the current, second-hand value of the entire contents is likely to be minimal. It may have cost several thousand pounds or more to purchase the contents originally, but their current second-hand value is the value that the court will use. Accordingly, you will not want to spend a substantial sum on legal costs arguing over the division of the contents. Again, equal division is the starting point (save for personal possessions, such as clothes, which each party should keep), although there will be other considerations, in particular if one party is to have any children living with them then their needs will obviously be greater. If you are not able to agree the division of the contents with your spouse, then my view is that all of the contents should remain in the matrimonial home until agreement is reached as to its division or the court has decided the matter. However, if your spouse starts removing items without your consent then you may be left with no alternative but to do likewise, especially in respect of items that you would like to keep or items that may be liquidated by your spouse.

WHY AN ORDER IS REQUIRED

There are essentially two reasons why an order setting out any financial/property settlement is required: finality and enforceability. It is only when an order is made (and the divorce is finalised – the order doesn't take effect until then) that the settlement is final, so far as possible. For example, if it is a 'clean-break' order (that is, with no ongoing liability or potential liability for one spouse to pay maintenance to the other), then the court will make an order dismissing all further financial/property claims by either party against the other or the other's estate. Only when such an order is made can you be sure that your spouse cannot make any further financial/property claim against you.

As to enforceability, any settlement is worthless if the other party refuses to give effect to it, even if it is agreed. The only way that you can enforce it (see the end of this chapter) is to have it incorporated into an order, and enforcing the order. The order will specify time limits for implementing the settlement, for example a time limit by which a lump sum should be paid – if that time limit is not met, then you can ask the court to enforce the order.

The other thing to mention here is the 'remarriage trap'. This refers to the rule that if you remarry then you cannot make a financial/property claim in respect of your previous marriage. If you have made such a claim, then remarriage doesn't prevent you from proceeding with that claim. The remarriage trap should only concern you if you are the respondent in undefended divorce proceedings, as any claim made in a divorce petition or answer counts. The simplest rule, though, is not to remarry until a financial/property (ancillary relief) order has been made, unless you take legal advice.

TYPES OF ORDER

There are four main types of order that the court can make.

Maintenance orders

These order that one spouse pays maintenance (periodical payments) to the other spouse. These orders are comparatively rare, as the court will try wherever possible to achieve a clean break (see above). Spousal maintenance orders generally fall into one of three categories:

■ Long-term orders, possibly lasting for the rest of the payer's/ recipient's life. These are usually made where one spouse is financially dependent on the other spouse and is unlikely ever to achieve financial independence. For example, after a long marriage where the recipient spouse is unable to work due to age or disability.

■ Short-term orders, designed to last long enough to enable the recipient spouse to establish (or re-establish) their financial independence. These may last, for example, for a period of two years.

■ Nominal orders, whereby one spouse pays a purely nominal sum (say, five pence per annum) to the other spouse. The purpose of such orders is to leave open the possibility of the recipient spouse applying to the court at some point in the future for the maintenance to be increased, should their circumstances change (that is, no clean break). These orders are favoured by many district judges where there are minor children – the court will make a nominal maintenance order in favour of the party looking after the children, with the order lasting until the children grow up/finish education. The idea here is that the order enables the court to award maintenance to that party should circumstances require this (for example, that party losing their job), the court having no power to make a child maintenance order because of the child support system.

Note that the amount of a maintenance order is not fixed in stone – it can be varied (upwards or downwards) at any point in the future, should there be a change in either party's circumstances. It is also possible to have the amount of the maintenance index-linked, so that, for example, it automatically changes each year in line with the Retail Prices Index. An example of index-linked maintenance (for children) can be found in paragraphs 6 and 7 of the example separation agreement in Appendix 1.

Maintenance for a spouse will always end when either spouse dies (although if the payer dies then the recipient can usually make a claim against the payer's estate), or when the recipient spouse remarries (note that the recipient spouse cohabiting with another person does *not* automatically end the maintenance, although it may be grounds for it to be reduced, possibly to a nominal amount). Otherwise, the maintenance will last as long as the order specifies or until the court orders otherwise.

One final point on the subject of maintenance, and it applies to the entire financial/property settlement. Contrary to popular belief, the law does *not* favour husband or wife. The fact that most spousal maintenance orders are in favour of wives is simply due to the fact that wives are more often financially dependent upon husbands, and more often the primary carers for any minor children.

Lump sum orders

These order that one spouse pay a lump sum of money to the other spouse, whether in one go or by instalments. As mentioned below, the order may be connected with an order requiring the recipient to transfer their interest in property, in particular the former matrimonial home, to the payer.

Property adjustment orders

These are, literally, orders adjusting the ownership of matrimonial property. Most commonly relating to the matrimonial home, a property adjustment order can, for example, alter the parties' shares in the property from 50/50 to 60/40 or whatever proportions the court considers appropriate. The court can even order one party to transfer their entire share in the property to the other party, possibly in return for a lump sum. If necessary, the court can also order a sale of property, so that the respective shares of the parties can be realised. Where one party needs to stay in the property, for example so that they can remain there with the children, the court can also order a sale at some point in the future, such as when the children have grown up or when the party in the property remarries or cohabits with another person.

Pension orders

There are two types of pension orders that the court can make: pension attachment orders and pension sharing orders. A pension attachment order will state that one party will receive part of the other party's pension *when the other party receives it*. These orders are not very satisfactory, as the receiving party has to wait until the other party takes their pension, and so they are now quite rare.

A pension sharing order, on the other hand, takes effect immediately (or as soon as it is implemented by the pension provider) and means that one party will receive all or part of the other party's pension, by way of a transfer of all or part of the pension fund into a pension in the receiving party's name. Note that this does *not* mean that the receiving party will get a lump sum of money from the other party's pension provider – they will just get a credit paid into their pension (they may have to set up a new pension for this purpose) and they will not receive any money themselves until their pension comes into payment. The same 50/50 starting-point applies to pension sharing, although it is arguable that any proportion of the pension that was accumulated prior to the marriage should be left out of account. Lastly, note that most pension providers will charge a fee for implementing a pension sharing order and this will be payable by the holder of the original pension, unless agreed/ordered otherwise.

There is, in fact, a third way of dealing with pensions and this is usually referred to as 'offsetting'. Under offsetting, the party with the pension will keep the pension, with the other party being compensated by receiving a greater share of other assets. Obviously, offsetting is only an option where there are other assets of similar value available.

IF TERMS ARE AGREED – CONSENT ORDERS

If the parties are able to agree a financial/property settlement, then they will need to have the agreement incorporated into a consent court order. It is normally possible to obtain such an order through the post, without the necessity for a court hearing, although, as will be seen, the court will require a few brief details of each party's means and circumstances to ensure that the order it is being asked to make is broadly reasonable. Note that the court does *not* have to make the order simply because the parties agree to its terms – if the court is not happy that the terms are reasonable, then it can refuse to make the order.

Applying for a consent order

This entails drafting the order, agreeing the draft with the other party and filing it with the court. Obviously, drafting a court order is not really something that a layperson can be expected to do, although there is an example of a simple consent order to be found in Appendix 1. If neither party has a solicitor, then one party will need to instruct a solicitor to prepare the draft order. If your spouse has a solicitor, then they may draft the order and send it to you for approval, but in view of the technicalities I would advise that you consult a solicitor before approving the draft.

Once the wording of the draft order has been agreed by both parties, it is signed by them and by any solicitors acting for either party.

The court will also require each party to complete a statement of information for a consent order form. The purpose of this form is to inform the court of each party's circumstances, so that the court can decide whether or not the order it is being asked to make is broadly reasonable, as mentioned above. An example of the form can also be found in Appendix 1.

In addition, the court will require both parties to complete a Form A –application for ancillary relief, for dismissal purposes. This is basically an application for all types of financial/property settlement order, the point being that until such an application is made, the court cannot dismiss those claims in the consent order (thereby ensuring the settlement is final). An example of Form A can also be found in Appendix 1. When filing this with a consent order, add the words 'For Dismissal Purposes Only' to the top of the front page.

Once all of the documents are ready, they are filed with the court along with the £40 court fee, which is usually shared. The court will then consider the papers and make the order if it is satisfied that its terms are reasonable. The court will date and seal the order and send copies to both sides. If the court wants any further information before making the order, it will notify the party who filed the papers.

Note that the order does not take effect until decree absolute. Accordingly, if you have not already applied for the decree absolute, you should do so now.

IF TERMS ARE NOT AGREED – CONTESTED APPLICATIONS

If you are unable to agree a financial/property settlement with your spouse, whether directly, through solicitors or via mediation, then the only way to resolve the matter will be for one party to make an application to the court, requesting the court to decide the issue – known as an 'application for ancillary relief'. Somewhat confusingly, the party making the application will be known as 'the applicant', and the other party will be known as 'the respondent', even if they are the petitioner in the divorce proceedings.

Before making the application, the applicant (and indeed the respondent) should be aware of the pre-application protocol, which essentially obliges both parties to make a reasonable effort to settle the matter by agreement before an application is made, including voluntarily disclosing details of their means to the other party. Failure to comply with the protocol could have consequences in any subsequent application, such as the court ordering the non-complying party to pay costs.

Application for ancillary relief

The procedure on an application for ancillary relief is detailed but is essentially quite straightforward as Figure 4.1 makes clear.

To go into a little more detail, the applicant commences the procedure by filing a Form A – application for ancillary relief with the court. An example Form A can be found in Appendix 1. As will be seen, it is a fairly simple document; the only slight complication being whether or not you were the petitioner in the divorce. If you were, then you should have included financial/ property claims in the prayer of your petition, in which case the Form A signifies your intention to proceed with those claims. If you were the respondent in the divorce, then the Form A is your original application for a financial/property settlement. Otherwise, you just fill in the case details, the respondent's address, tick all six boxes for what you want to claim, insert the address of any property involved (that is, the former matrimonial home) in the box, sign and date the form. You then file the form with the court, together with a copy for the respondent and the court fee, which is currently £210.

The court will then draw up a timetable for the application to proceed. This involves three matters. Firstly, the court will fix a

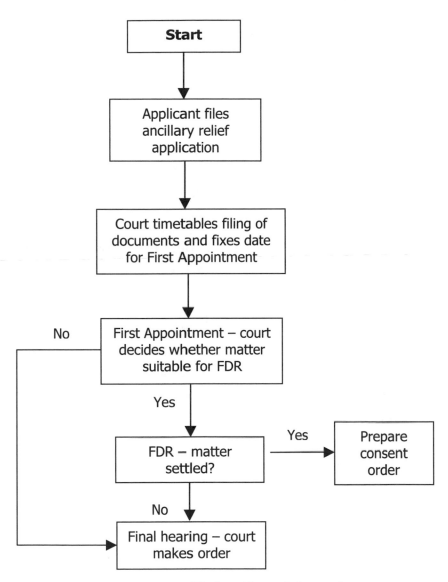

Figure 4.1 Simplified ancillary relief procedure

First Appointment date, not less than 12 weeks and not more than 16 weeks after the date the Form A is filed. Secondly, the court will set a date by when each party must file and serve a detailed financial statement (Form E – see below), which will be not less than 35 days before the First Appointment. Thirdly, the court will set a date (at least 14 days before the First Appointment), by when each party must file and serve other required documents, which I will detail below. The timetable will be written into a notice of a First Appointment, which the court will send to both parties, together with the sealed Form A.

When the applicant receives the papers back from the court, they should also serve copies upon the respondent to ensure that they have received them. In addition, copies should be served on any mortgagee of any property involved (that is, the bank or building society to whom the former matrimonial home is mortgaged), the landlord if the property is rented, and the other party's pension provider if a pension order is being sought and their details are known. Even if a pension sharing order is not being sought, if either party has a pension then they must, within seven days of receiving notification of the date of the First Appointment, apply to their pension provider for information regarding the pension, including a cash equivalent transfer valuation (CETV) of the pension (if they have not already got one that is dated not earlier than 12 months prior to the date of the First Appointment), and details of any charges that the provider would make to implement a pension sharing order. The provider must supply this information within six weeks of receiving the request. The party requesting the information must then send it to the other party, within seven days of receipt. (Note that if it is decided that a pension attachment or pension sharing order is appropriate then additional information may be required about the pension arrangement, in which case a pension enquiry form (Form P, available on the Courts Service website) may be sent to the pension provider. The court may order this to be done.)

The rest of the ancillary relief procedure is detailed below but to finish this summary: the parties must comply with the timetable directed by the court, and then both attend the First Appointment, the purpose of which is to define the issues and decide how the matter is to proceed. The next stage in the procedure is usually a Financial Dispute Resolution appointment (FDR), at which the parties should use their best endeavours to settle the matter by agreement, with the help of the court. Only if they cannot reach agreement will the court fix a date for a final, contested hearing.

Form E – Financial statement

Right, take a deep breath, get yourself a cup of tea and make yourself comfortable. Form E can be a daunting document to complete. However, it is mostly self-explanatory, so the following does not explain every section in detail.

Before you begin, you should gather together all of the information and documentation that you will need to complete the form. In particular, copies of the following documents (and, generally, no others) must be attached to the form:

■ Any valuation obtained in the last six months of the matrimonial home or any other land or property, plus the latest mortgage statement, confirming the amount outstanding.

■ Bank and building society statements for the last 12 months, in respect of any account in which you have had an interest during that period.

- The latest statement or dividend counterfoil relating to any investments held by you, such as shares.

- Surrender valuations for any life (endowment) policies that have a surrender value – these can be obtained from the insurance companies.

- The last two years' accounts for any business in which you have an interest and any document that is available to confirm the current value of that business, such as a letter from an accountant or a formal valuation if that has been obtained.

- As mentioned above, a cash equivalent transfer valuation (CETV) in the last 12 months for each pension arrangement, or a letter of request asking for that valuation.

- Your last three payslips and most recent P60, in respect of each employment that you have.

- Your last form P11D, if you have been issued with one.

- If you are self-employed, a copy of your last tax assessment or, if that is not available, a letter from your accountant confirming your tax liability. Further, if your net income from the last financial year and the estimated income for the next 12 months is significantly different, a copy of the management accounts for the period since your last accounts.

As mentioned above, the form is not explained here in detail but you should note the following:

1   If possible, you must fill in all of the form and attach all of the essential documents mentioned above (see also the schedule at the back of the form), as failure to do so could result in

delay and additional expense. If you are not able to obtain any of the documents within the time limit set by the court, then tick the 'to follow' box on the schedule and forward copies of those documents to the court and the other party as soon as they are to hand.

2   Section 1.13 – If there is no child support assessment and child maintenance has not been agreed, the estimate should be based upon the formula used by the Child Support Agency: normally 15% of the non-residential parent's net weekly income for one child, 20% for two children and 25% for three or more children. For more details, see Chapter 3. If you do not know the non-residential parent's income, then state this.

3   Section 2.1 – If the matrimonial home is owned jointly, then the value of your interest will be one half of the equity (i.e. the value less the amount outstanding under the mortgage and costs of sale).

4   Section 2.5 – As mentioned above, if the policy has a surrender value, then you will need to request this from the insurance company, if you do not have it already.

5   Section 2.16 – Again, as mentioned above, you will need to obtain a CETV from your pension provider. You may wish to send a copy of this page to your pension provider and ask them to complete it. If you have more than one pension, then you should complete a separate page for each pension.

6   Sections 2.15 to 2.19 – You must ensure that you give details of your income for all years requested.

7   Section 2.20 and 2.21 – Just transpose the figures from the relevant sections of the statement and complete the totals.

8   Section 3.1 – Give details of all of your regular outgoings, including mortgage repayments, council tax, insurances, gas, electricity and telephone bills, food, clothing, petrol, and so on.

9   Section 3.2 – Typical capital needs include housing (i.e. how much you would need to buy a suitable house for yourself), furniture required for your new home and the cost of a new car.

10   Section 4.4 – As stated in the notes, conduct will only affect the financial/property settlement if it is exceptional. For example, adultery is *not* exceptional. *Only* give details of conduct if it is exceptional – in most cases, conduct will not be an issue that will affect the financial/property settlement.

11   Section 5.1 – You may not be able to specify what kind of orders you will be asking the court to make, especially if you do not yet have details of your spouse's means. If this is the case, then just state 'I am not yet able to specify what order or orders I want the court to make'. If you are certain that you know what orders you want the court to make (for example, equal division of the assets and a clean break), then set out what you want here.

12   Sections 5.2 and 5.3 – You will not need to complete these sections, as they are not relevant to you.

Once you have completed the Form E you will need to attach the essential documents and have it sworn. This can be done either at the divorce court or in front of a solicitor (not belonging to the firm acting for the other party). The court office will be open from 10am to 4pm Mondays to Fridays, and they will not charge a fee for this service. If you take the form to a solicitor, you will be charged a fee of £5.

Once the Form E has been sworn, you should file the original (with attached documents) with the court. You will also need to serve a copy upon the other party or their solicitors. The forms are usually exchanged simultaneously, so get in touch with the other party or their solicitor, inform them that your Form E is ready for exchange and, if theirs is also ready, each party will agree to send a copy of their form to the other in the post that day. Make sure that you keep a copy of your form for yourself.

OTHER REQUIRED DOCUMENTS

You must now file with the court certain documentation, comprising the following:

1 A **chronology**, setting out briefly the history of the matter. An example chronology can be found in Appendix 1. As can be seen, it is a fairly simple document.

2 A **concise statement** of the apparent issues between yourself and your spouse, i.e. the matters that the court will have to decide. Again, an example statement is included in Appendix 1. Be sure only to include issues that are relevant to the financial/ property settlement, such as those set out in the example. You should get a good idea of the relevant issues by reading your spouse's Form E, particularly Section 5.1. For example, is there any dispute about the assets of each party? Perhaps you think that the other party has undervalued or even failed to disclose

their assets or income. Is there a dispute as to whether or not one party is cohabiting or intends to cohabit? Is one party claiming that they have contributed more to the marriage than the other party? Then you need to consider what each party is asking for. For example, should there be a clean break? Should there be an unequal division of assets? Should there be a pension sharing order? Do *not* include issues that are not relevant to the financial/property settlement, for example the reasons for the breakdown of the marriage are rarely relevant – there is nothing more guaranteed to annoy the district judge than wasting their time with irrelevant matters.

3   A **questionnaire** setting out the further information and documents that you require from your spouse. Again, an example questionnaire can be found in Appendix 1. In particular, you should check whether there are any matters that are not correct in your spouse's Form E or any matters that they have omitted from the form – if so, these matters should be raised in the questionnaire. Please note, however, that the questionnaire can only contain questions that are relevant to the outcome of the matter, and that the court will consider whether the questions are relevant at the First Appointment (see below). You do not therefore need to reply to the other party's questionnaire prior to the First Appointment.

4   A **Form G** – notice of response to First Appointment, on which you must state whether or not you will be in a position to proceed with a Financial Dispute Resolution (FDR) appointment (see below), at the First Appointment. Appendix 1 includes an example Form G. Most often, you will not be in a position to proceed with a FDR at the First Appointment because you will still be requiring further disclosure from the

other party, in particular in reply to your questionnaire. In any event, the matter is often academic because the court will often not have enough time available to proceed with an FDR at the First Appointment.

Once these four documents are ready, you must file them with the court and serve copies upon the other party within the time limit set out by the court.

When you receive copies of your spouse's documents, you should obviously read them, paying particular attention to their statement of issues and questionnaire. Consider whether any of the issues can be resolved by agreement, thereby reducing the number of matters that the court has to decide. As to their questionnaire, you do not yet have to reply to it, as mentioned above. However, consider whether any of the questions are irrelevant (or have already been answered), in which case you can ask the court to disallow those questions, at the First Appointment.

THE FIRST APPOINTMENT

Both parties must attend the First Appointment. The objective of the Appointment is to define the issues and save costs. Obviously, the fewer the issues between the parties, the less the costs are likely to be. You may think that this is not relevant to you if you are not instructing a solicitor, but you may be ordered to pay the other party's costs if you do not conduct the case in a reasonable fashion (see Chapter 7), and you may wish to instruct a solicitor to represent you at any final hearing – see below.

The First Appointment is usually conducted in a fairly informal fashion. No evidence will be taken from the parties and the court will not make a final order, unless a settlement is agreed between the parties. The only time that the court will make an order (apart from the directions mentioned below) is where one party is asking for an interim order, such as maintenance pending suit, i.e. a temporary maintenance order that will last until a final order is made.

The matters that the district judge will deal with at the First Appointment will include the following:

■ What questions in each party's questionnaire the other party must answer, as mentioned above. The district judge will strike out any irrelevant questions and will then direct that each party must reply to the rest of the other party's questionnaire by a specific date. (Replies should also be filed with the court.)

■ Whether there is any dispute over valuations of assets and, if so, how that dispute is to be resolved. For example, if the parties are in dispute as to the value of the former matrimonial home, then the court will usually direct that there be a joint valuation, i.e. the parties will jointly instruct a single expert (and will be bound by their valuation), sharing the expert's fees.

■ Whether the case is suitable to be referred to a Financial Dispute Resolution appointment (assuming the First Appointment is not also being used as an FDR) and, if so, fixing a date for the FDR. If the case is not appropriate for an FDR, then the district judge will either fix another directions hearing or will fix a date for the final hearing, unless the parties have agreed to go to out-of-court mediation, in which case the proceedings will be adjourned for long enough for the mediation to take place.

Note that neither party is entitled to produce any further documents, save as directed by the court. Accordingly, if there are any other documents that you wish to produce, then you must ask the court for permission to do so. (If, after the First Appointment, either party wants the court to make any further directions, then they will need to request another directions appointment.)

FINANCIAL DISPUTE RESOLUTION APPOINTMENT

Once again, both parties must attend the Financial Dispute Resolution (FDR) appointment. The FDR appointment 'must be treated as a meeting held for the purposes of discussion and negotiation'. In other words, the idea of the FDR appointment is for the parties to use their best endeavours to settle the matter by agreement, with the help of the court. As part of this process, the party that issued the application for ancillary relief must, not less than seven days before the FDR, file with the court details of all offers or proposals made by either party (even without prejudice offers – see glossary), together with the other party's responses to them.

The FDR appointment is usually conducted quite informally. The district judge hearing the appointment will usually indicate his or her views as to what final order is likely to be appropriate, and can advise the parties that the costs implications make it sensible to examine how the gap between them can be bridged. Note, however, that the court cannot impose a settlement upon the parties at the FDR appointment. Note also that, to ensure that the parties approach the appointment openly, anything said at the appointment (including any offers disclosed) is not admissible in any subsequent proceedings. In addition, the judge conducting the appointment will play no further part in the proceedings.

If the parties are able to reach a full agreement at the FDR appointment, then a consent court order can be drawn up, signed by the parties and handed in to the court, in much the same way as the consent orders referred to above. If there is not time to draw up the order, then written heads of agreement (i.e. an outline of the agreement) can be signed by the parties and handed to the judge, with a full order filed later.

If no agreement is reached at the FDR appointment, then the court will fix a date for a final, contested hearing and give any other directions that it considers appropriate.

THE FINAL HEARING

A considerable amount of preparation is required prior to a final hearing including, in particular, the preparation of a bundle of documents for the court, including specific documents required by the rules. At the hearing the court will hear evidence from both parties (and their witnesses), under oath, and the other party or their legal representative will be able to cross examine. The hearing is conducted in a strictly formal way. In view of these things, it can be a daunting prospect for many litigants acting in person (i.e. representing themselves). Accordingly, I would recommend that if the case reaches this stage, you should seriously consider whether you wish to instruct a solicitor to represent you at the hearing. If you do, you should instruct the solicitor as soon as possible to give them the best opportunity to prepare the case for you.

If you do decide to continue to represent yourself, then the first thing you should do when the final hearing date is fixed is read the practice direction on court bundles dated 27 July 2006, which can be found on the Courts Service website (www.hmcourts-service.gov.uk). This explains what documents are required in the bundle and when it should be filed with the court.

As to the hearing itself, I can give little specific advice, as what to do and say will of course depend upon the facts of your case. I will, however, give two pieces of general advice. Firstly, prepare well for the hearing – make sure you are aware of those issues that are relevant to the outcome of the case and that you know exactly what order or orders you will be asking the court to make. Secondly, at the hearing, keep what you say and ask relevant to the issues – as I've said before, there is nothing worse than upsetting the judge by wasting their time going through irrelevant matters. Even if you do not want to instruct a solicitor to represent you at the hearing, you may wish to take some advice from a solicitor to clarify exactly what issues are relevant to the outcome of the case.

Once all the evidence has been heard, the district judge will make his or her decision. If there is time, and if the district judge does not want time to consider matters, the decision will be given at the end of the hearing, otherwise the hearing will be adjourned and you will need to go back to court on another day to hear the decision. The decision will be written up into a court order, a copy of which you will receive. Note once again that the order will only take effect when the divorce is finalised (if it has not been finalised already), by the decree absolute.

IMPLEMENTING THE ORDER

The following applies equally to orders made by the court after a contested hearing and to orders made by consent. Obviously, what needs to be done to implement the order depends upon the contents of the order, but here are some examples:

- An order for payment of a lump sum – the party required to pay the lump sum must pay it to the other party within the time limit set down by the court. Failure to do so could result in the paying party incurring interest (which may be specified in the order) and further costs.

- An order for the transfer of property – often simultaneously with the payment of a lump sum by the transferee to the transferor. The transferor will need to do everything necessary to transfer their interest in the property to the transferee, within the time limit specified by the court. If any real property, such as the former matrimonial home, is to be transferred to you, then you will need to instruct a solicitor to deal with the conveyancing. Even if you are the transferring party, you would do well to seek legal advice upon the transfer document, for example to ensure that you are being released from any mortgage on the property.

- Pension sharing orders – a copy of the order with pension sharing annex will have to be sent to the other party's pension provider, with a request that they implement the order. (You will need to take independent financial advice about setting up a pension into which the pension share is to be transferred.) You (and/or the other party, depending upon the terms of the order) will also need to pay any fee required by the pension provider for implementing the order, and the pension provider will also need to see a copy of the decree absolute to ensure that the order has taken effect.

■ Orders relating to endowment policies – these may be sold/surrendered (and the proceeds divided) or one party may be required to transfer (or assign) their interest in the policy to the other party. An appropriate deed of assignment can usually be obtained from the insurance company, which is then signed and returned to the company with a request that the company give effect to the assignment.

A SHORT NOTE ABOUT APPEALS

Appealing ancillary relief orders is beyond the scope of this book. Suffice to say that the grounds for appealing these orders is very limited and you should therefore seek legal advice if you are considering an appeal. Remember that if your appeal fails, then you are likely to be ordered to pay the other party's costs of the appeal, which are likely to be substantial. Remember also that an appeal should usually be lodged within 14 days of the date of the order being appealed against, so you will need to act quickly, although it is possible to appeal out of time.

It is also possible to apply to have an order set aside, where essential facts were not disclosed to the court by the other party. In addition, you can, in limited circumstances, appeal against an order out of time where new events occur shortly after the making of the order which fundamentally alter the basis of the order (for example, a substantial change in the value of an asset). Again, in either instance you should seek legal advice before proceeding.

ENFORCING ORDERS

What if one party fails to comply with the terms of the order? Well, the other party will then have to take enforcement action. Enforcement is a subject in itself, so all eventualities are not dealt with here (nor are the procedural details), but here are some of the most common possibilities:

- Unpaid maintenance orders – if the paying party is employed, then you can apply for an attachment of earnings order, requiring their employer to deduct the maintenance from their earnings, in much the same way that the Child Support Agency can make a deduction from earnings order, as mentioned in Chapter 3.

- Failure to pay a lump sum – this can be enforced against the payer in the same ways as any civil debt, for example by seeking a garnishee order, requiring their bank to pay the money from their bank account, or by seeking a charging order, attaching the debt to their property and thereafter, if necessary, requiring the property to be sold to pay the debt, or by seeking a warrant of execution, whereby their goods are seized and sold to pay the debt.

- Failure to comply with a transfer of property order – here, you can apply to the court for an order that the district judge sign any documents required to give effect to the transfer, for example a document transferring one party's interest in the former matrimonial home to the other party.

As usual, if you are in any doubt as to what to do to enforce an order, then you should seek legal advice.

5

Domestic Violence

If you are a victim of domestic violence then you will probably want to instruct a solicitor to represent you. This chapter will not therefore go into as much detail as other chapters. However, many victims are not eligible for legal aid and cannot afford to instruct a solicitor. This chapter is therefore designed to give basic help to such people and also those who are accused of domestic violence. Note that criminal matters are not discussed (save in relation to breaches of court orders), as they are beyond the scope of this book.

WHAT IS DOMESTIC VIOLENCE?

The first thing to emphasise is that 'domestic violence' does not just include physical violence. The government defines domestic violence as 'Any incident of threatening behaviour, violence or abuse (psychological, physical, sexual, financial or emotional) between adults who are or have been intimate partners or family members, regardless of gender or sexuality.' Accordingly, it includes such things as making threats, verbal abuse, harassment and even withholding money.

CHANGING THE LOCKS

A question that I have regularly been asked over the years is: 'My spouse has left the matrimonial home – can I change the locks to prevent them returning?' The answer really depends upon whose *home* it is. If one spouse excludes the other then the excluded spouse can apply to a court for an order requiring the first spouse to allow him/her back into the property. However, if the property is clearly no longer the excluded spouse's home then the court is unlikely to make such an order (save, perhaps, to allow the excluded party back briefly to collect their belongings), even where the excluded spouse is a legal owner of the property.

Note that if the excluded spouse forces entry into the property while the other spouse is in occupation then they may be committing a criminal offence, even if they are a legal owner of the property and no occupation order has been made (see below). Even if the other spouse is not in occupation, a court is likely to take a dim view of such behaviour.

COURT ORDERS AVAILABLE

A victim of domestic violence can apply for an injunction order, which is an order requiring a party to do, or to refrain from doing, certain acts. There are two main types of injunction available: non-molestation orders and occupation orders.

A **non-molestation order** is aimed at preventing your spouse from using or threatening violence against you or your child, or intimidating, harassing or pestering you, in order to ensure the health, safety and well-being of yourself and your children.

An **occupation order** regulates who can live in the matrimonial home and can also restrict your spouse from entering the surrounding area. If you do not feel safe continuing to live with your spouse or if you have left home because of violence, but want to return and exclude your spouse, you may want to apply for an occupation order.

While getting a court order may provide some protection, it isn't always helpful: sometimes it makes very little difference and it can even (in some cases) be counter-productive. You should therefore consider whether seeking an order is the best course of action for you, before proceeding. For example, are you prepared for your spouse to go to prison if they breach the order? If not, then the order is virtually worthless. Is your spouse going to pay any attention to the order or even likely to react violently to it? I'm not for one moment suggesting that anyone should submit to domestic violence but I've seen many cases where applicants have found themselves no safer, or even less safe, after an order has been made. Sometimes, the best course of action is simply to take practical steps to protect yourself, for example getting away from your spouse or going straight to the police for protection.

The order will last for a specified period (which the applicant can subsequently ask the court to extend) or until the court makes a further order.

APPLYING FOR AN ORDER

An application for a non-molestation and/or occupation order is made to the court where the divorce proceedings are taking place. The applicant files with the court an application in Form

FL401 (available on the Courts Service website – www.hmcourts-service.gov.uk), together with a sworn statement, setting out the grounds of the application. A court fee of £60 is payable. The applicant should also file a draft of the order that they are seeking (see Form FL404).

After the application is filed, the court will fix a hearing date and issue a notice of proceedings with the date on it. The applicant will then have to arrange for the respondent to be personally served with the notice, together with copies of the application and sworn statement, not less than two days before the hearing date (the court can shorten this time in cases of emergency). After service, a statement of service (Form FL415) must be filed with the court.

Urgent applications

If the applicant is in immediate danger, an application can be made to the court on the same day without the respondent being there. This is known as a without notice application. The court will need to consider whether or not the applicant is at risk of significant harm, whether they will be prevented or deterred from applying if they have to wait or whether the respondent is avoiding being served with the papers.

If the court grants a without notice order, it will fix a date for a full hearing, as soon as just and convenient. The applicant will then have to arrange for the respondent to be personally served with the order and other papers, as above. Note that the without notice order will not take effect until the respondent has been served with it.

If there are other family proceedings already in progress (for example, for a residence or contact order for a child) the court may wish to hear the whole case together – but they can still grant a without notice order while the applicant is waiting for the full hearing.

RESPONDING TO AN APPLICATION

If the respondent objects to the making of an order, then they will need to file a sworn statement in reply to the applicant's allegations and attend the full hearing to oppose the application. However, they would be advised to consider whether or not it is worth opposing the application. The considerations differ, depending upon which type of order the applicant is seeking:

A **non-molestation order**: Such an order is, of course, only ordering you to refrain from doing what you should not do anyway, i.e. molest the applicant. In this light, the only thing you have to lose if the order is made is any costs that the court may order you to pay. You may, therefore, consider offering an undertaking to the court not to molest the applicant (see below) on the basis that the court makes no order for costs against you.

An **occupation order**: Here, you need to take the long view. If the marriage has broken down, then you and your spouse will obviously have to separate at some point. That being the case, the question is: who should remain in the matrimonial home? If there are children, and it is clear that they should live primarily with the applicant, then it may be the case that that you will have to vacate the property at some time in the near future, in which case it would be pointless opposing the application. On the other hand, if there are no children, then it may be that the property will have to be sold soon, in which case there may be little practical point in opposing the application. Of course, all this presupposes that the applicant is seeking an order that you leave the property. If they are only seeking an order that you allow them back into the property, such an order is likely to be made anyway, unless they have (voluntarily) been away from the property for some considerable time.

THE HEARING

Both parties must attend the full hearing, which will usually be conducted by a district judge. The district judge will hear the evidence, and decide what order or orders to make. If they make an occupation order and they find that the respondent has used or threatened violence, they will attach a power of arrest to the order, unless, exceptionally, they are satisfied that the applicant will be adequately protected without it. A power of arrest means that a copy of the order must be held on record at the police station, and the police can arrest the respondent immediately if the order is broken, even without a criminal offence having been committed. A power of arrest may be attached even if the hearing was held without notice, if the court believes the applicant is likely to be at risk of harm otherwise.

The respondent may offer to the court an undertaking (or promise) not to molest the applicant, for example if they deny the allegations made by the applicant. The court can then accept the undertaking, without making any finding against the respondent. (Obviously, the court can take action against the respondent if they were to breach the undertaking). However, the court will not accept the undertaking if the respondent has used or threatened violence against the applicant (or a child) and for the protection of the applicant (or child) it is necessary to make a non-molestation order so that any breach will be punishable as a criminal offence (see below). The respondent could also offer an undertaking to vacate the matrimonial home, but the court will not accept the undertaking if it considers that there should be a power of arrest (see above), as a power of arrest cannot be attached to an undertaking.

IF AN ORDER IS BREACHED

A breach of a non-molestation order is a criminal offence. If the respondent breaches the terms of the order, and the police are called, they may arrest the respondent and treat the breach in the same way as any other criminal offence. The maximum sentence for the offence is five years imprisonment, although the sentence for a first offender is obviously likely to be considerably less.

If the respondent breaches an occupation order then they will have to be brought back before the same court that made the order (rather than a criminal court, as in the case of breach of a non-molestation order) for contempt of court. The court may then fine them, impose a suspended sentence or commit them to prison, which would be rare for a first offence. If a power of arrest is attached to the occupation order, then the police may arrest the respondent and bring them back before the court. If there is no power of arrest, then the applicant will have to bring them back to the court, by making an application for their committal to prison. The applicant can also apply for a warrant for the respondent's arrest.

Note that the respondent cannot both be guilty of a criminal offence *and* punished for contempt of court, in respect of the same conduct.

6

Mediation

WHAT IS MEDIATION?

Mediation is a process whereby a trained mediator will help a divorcing or separating couple agree arrangements for children and/or a financial/property settlement. The mediator will try to guide the parties in the right direction and will seek to ensure that neither party tries to bully the other into agreeing to unfavourable terms. If one party persists in such behaviour, then the mediator will bring the process to an end.

Note that mediators are not necessarily lawyers but, even if they are not, their training includes a knowledge of the law. However, some non-lawyer mediators may have insufficient knowledge if the case involves complex issues. On occasion, a non-lawyer mediator may not prevent the parties from reaching an unfair settlement or a settlement that is incomplete or includes terms that cannot legally be implemented. If this occurs, the matter will be picked up either by one of the parties' lawyers if that party takes legal advice upon the terms of the settlement, or by the court – see below.

Mediation is purely voluntary. Accordingly, you cannot go to mediation unless your spouse agrees. Furthermore, either party may withdraw from the mediation process at any time.

DOES IT COST ANYTHING?

Yes. Mediation is not free, but the fees involved are generally substantially less than the cost of solicitors and contested court proceedings. The fees are usually shared equally between the parties. Fee amounts vary from one mediation agency to another and depend upon how long the mediation process takes. Check on the fee amount before instructing a mediator.

HOW DOES MEDIATION WORK?

The exact process will vary from one mediation agency to another, and possibly from one case to another, depending upon what is involved. However, the process will usually begin by one party contacting the agency and the agency sending out a referral form for them to complete. The referral form will contain basic details of both parties and any children involved, and a brief summary of the issues that need to be resolved.

If the agency is being asked to mediate upon financial/property issues following divorce it will usually require both parties to complete a means form before the mediation itself begins, as obviously the mediator will need full details of the means of both parties in order to mediate. If the mediator believes that one of the parties has not made a full disclosure of their means, then they should request such disclosure and, if it is not forthcoming, should end the mediation process.

Once the preliminaries have been dealt with, the mediation process itself begins. This will comprise one or (usually) more 'round-table' meetings between the parties and the mediator.

Obviously, the number of meetings and amount of time spent will depend upon the complexity of the issues and the willingness of the parties to negotiate. However, if the mediator should believe that the issues are incapable of resolution then they will bring the mediation process to an end.

If the mediation process is successful, the mediator will make a written record of the agreement, usually called 'Heads of Agreement', and will send a copy to each party.

AGREEMENTS ARE NOT FINAL

It is important to note that an agreement reached in mediation *is not final*. Each party may then seek legal advice upon the terms of the agreement (as they can at any point in the process). Once again, if the agreement is regarding a financial settlement the lawyer will require details of both parties' means before they can advise. As indicated above, the lawyer should advise not only upon whether the agreement is fair but also upon whether its terms are complete and can be legally implemented.

If, after taking advice (or even without taking advice), either party wishes to amend the agreement or withdraw from it completely, they may do so. If they do not withdraw completely then further negotiations may take place, with or without the mediator.

Once an agreement has been reached and confirmed by both parties, after they have had a reasonable opportunity to take legal advice, then the agreement will have to be implemented. How this happens will depend both upon the nature of the agreement, and whether or not there are court proceedings:

■ If the agreement relates only to arrangements for children and neither party has applied to the court for a residence or contact order (or any other order relating to children), then no steps are required to implement it, although if there are no divorce proceedings the terms may be included in a separation agreement – see the Introduction to this book.

■ If the agreement relates only to arrangements for children and either party has applied to the court for a residence or contact order (or any other order relating to children), then the agreement may be incorporated into a court order *if the court considers that an order is required*, for example to ensure that the parties keep to the terms of the agreement. Often, however, the court will not consider that an order is required – the no order principle – see Chapter 2.

■ If the agreement relates to finances and property and there are no divorce proceedings, then it should be incorporated into a separation agreement, as mentioned in the Introduction.

■ If the agreement relates to finances and property and there are divorce proceedings, then it should be incorporated into a consent court order, as explained in Chapter 4.

How do I find a mediator?

There are many mediation agencies spread around the country. To find one local to you, contact the Family Mediation Helpline on 0845 60 26 627 or at www.familymediationhelpline.co.uk. For further details, see Appendix 2.

7

Costs and Legal Aid

COSTS OF THE DIVORCE

Unfortunately, we still have a fault-based divorce system, at least until the parties have been separated for two years. This means that if the divorce is based upon adultery or unreasonable behaviour then the court will take the view that the breakdown of the marriage was the fault of the respondent (whether or not this was really the case), and order him/her to pay the petitioner's costs of the divorce, assuming that the petitioner has included a claim for costs in their petition.

Note that costs orders are not considered to be appropriate in five years' separation divorce cases, so if you claim costs in such a case you should not get your costs order. Point this out to the court on your acknowledgement form if you are the respondent in a five years' separation case and the petitioner has asked the court to order you to pay their costs.

COSTS IN CHILDREN PROCEEDINGS

Costs orders in proceedings relating to children are very rare, and will generally only be made against a party who has conducted the proceedings in an extremely unreasonable fashion and with no regard for the welfare of the children. Accordingly, if you are involved in children proceedings you should expect to have to pay your own costs even if you succeed in getting the order you seek. By the same token, if you do not succeed you should not be ordered to pay or contribute towards the other party's costs, unless you were clearly unreasonable in the way you conducted the proceedings.

COSTS IN FINANCIAL/PROPERTY PROCEEDINGS

The general rule in financial/property proceedings (ancillary relief) is that the court will not make an order requiring one party to pay the costs of the other party, but the court may make such an order at any stage in the proceedings if it considers it appropriate to do so because of the conduct of a party *in relation to the proceedings*, whether before (for example, failure to comply with the pre-application protocol – see Chapter 4) or during them. In deciding whether to make such an order, the court must have regard to the following:

a) Any failure by a party to comply with the rules, or with any order of the court, for example failure to do something within a time limit set by the court.

b) Any open offer (i.e. proposal) to settle by a party – an open offer is an offer not made without prejudice (i.e. the letter setting out the terms of the offer has the words 'without prejudice' at the top of it). The purpose of a without prejudice offer is to ensure that the offer cannot be shown to the court if it is not accepted, so that the recipient cannot use it to argue that the maker of the offer should pay at least that sum. It is usually used to make generous offers and, until the rules changed in 2006, was often used save as to costs (called a 'Calderbank' offer), so that if the offer was not accepted and it was not beaten in court, the maker of the offer could then show the letter to the court and ask the court to order the other party to pay their costs from the date of the offer, on the basis that those costs would have been saved if the offer had been accepted. However, for all proceedings started on or after 3 April 2006, the court no longer takes into account any offers headed 'without prejudice' or 'without prejudice save as to costs' when considering whether to make a costs order. Accordingly, if you want to ensure that the other party could be penalised in costs if they refuse your offer and then fail to beat it in court, then that offer must be made in an open letter. Open offers must obviously be carefully considered in the light of the possible costs consequences of failing to beat the offer in court – if a party is represented then their costs of a final hearing alone are likely to be at least £3,000, and very probably considerably more than that.

c) Whether it was reasonable for a party to raise, pursue or contest a particular allegation or issue – so make sure that any matter that you raise in the course of the proceedings is actually relevant to the outcome of the proceedings. For example, there is no point in a husband trying to prove that his wife has a boyfriend if there is no evidence that they have any intention of cohabiting. Similarly, there is no point in contesting an allegation made by the other party if they clearly have evidence that proves the allegation.

d) The manner in which a party has pursued or responded to the application or a particular allegation or issue, such as continual unwarranted requests for further information and/ or documentation – the 'fishing expedition' – in the hope of finding something to support your case or, worse still, taking or copying documents belonging to the other party without their permission.

e) Any other aspect of a party's conduct in relation to the proceedings which the court considers relevant – an example here might be threats made to the other party if they pursue their claim.

f) Lastly, the financial effect on the parties of any costs order.

QUANTIFYING COSTS

Generally speaking, costs orders will take one of two forms: either the court will quantify the costs when it makes the order, or it will order that either the costs are agreed between the parties (see below) or, if not agreed, they will be assessed by the court. Having costs assessed by the court involves preparing a detailed bill (in the required format) and sending it to the court for it to be assessed. The court will consider not just the rates charged, but also whether the work claimed was properly required to be done.

ENFORCING COSTS ORDERS

Once the amount of the costs has been quantified by the court, then the costs can be enforced in the same way as any other civil debt – see the section on enforcing orders in Chapter 4.

AGREED COSTS

If you need to agree your spouse's solicitor's costs, for example in advance of divorce proceedings or if you have been ordered to pay the costs, you will need to have some idea of reasonable hourly rates. The rates charged by solicitors vary depending upon the experience of the solicitor doing the work and the area in which they practice. So, for example, a senior solicitor practising in London is likely to charge more than any other solicitor practising in another part of the country. I can't give you rates for all solicitors in all parts of the country but, at the time of writing, I doubt that any solicitor charges less than £100 an hour for non-legal aid work, and the top solicitors can charge up to £600 an hour, although if more than £200 an hour is claimed, then you should seek an explanation.

As to the total cost of the job itself, this depends upon how much work is involved – most solicitors charge on the basis of the work that they do rather than on the basis of an estimate in advance. Having said that, some jobs can be given a reasonably accurate estimate. For example, a straightforward undefended divorce should cost no more than £1,000, and probably less.

In addition to the solicitor's costs (and VAT on them) you will, of course, need to include court fees and other reasonable disbursements.

AM I ELIGIBLE FOR LEGAL AID?

You will be eligible for legal aid if you are in receipt of income support. You may be eligible if you are on a low income and you have savings of less than £3,000. If you think you may be eligible for legal aid then you can check using the calculator on the Community Legal Advice website (www.communitylegaladvice. org.uk).

If you believe that you qualify for legal aid, then you should contact a family legal aid solicitor in your area. You can find a family legal aid solicitor by going to the 'Find a legal adviser' section on the Community Legal Advice website.

WHAT IF MY SPOUSE HAS LEGAL AID?

If your spouse has legal aid then their solicitors should notify you of this fact. Note that having legal aid does not necessarily mean that they will have no legal costs to pay. They may have a monthly contribution to pay towards their legal aid and they will have to repay their solicitor's costs out of any money or property that they recover or preserve (this is usually referred to as the 'legal aid charge'). If they recover or preserve an interest in the matrimonial home, then they will have to repay the legal aid charge when the home is sold.

The fact that your spouse has legal aid does not prevent the court from ordering you to pay all or part of their costs, and any such order would not be restricted to the lower rates that legal aid solicitors are usually paid. On the other hand, a legally aided person has substantial protection against costs orders being made against them, so that such orders are extremely rare. This can be seen as a considerable advantage for a legally aided person, particularly in negotiations, but remember that if the legal aid charge applies then it is just as much in their interests as yours to settle matters, in order to keep costs to a minimum.

Final Thoughts

CHECKLIST

Before you put away your file on the divorce, you should check that everything has been dealt with. In particular:

- Have you got your decree absolute?

- Have all arrangements for any children (with whom they will live and contact with the other parent, including holiday contact) been finalised? Remember that no order is required setting out these arrangements, if they are agreed.

- Has child maintenance been agreed, or dealt with by the Child Support Agency?

- Has a full financial/property settlement been agreed/ordered by the court? If it has been agreed, has a consent order, giving effect to the agreement, been made by the court?

- Lastly, have all the terms of the financial/property settlement been implemented? This will include payment of lump sums, transfers of property, implementation of pension sharing orders and dealing with any endowment policies.

EFFECT OF DIVORCE ON WILLS

Divorce does *not* have the effect of revoking existing wills (unlike marriage). If you have already made a will, then any reference in that will to your former spouse will be deleted. This can mean that all or part of the will will fail, possibly resulting in an intestacy, or a partial intestacy, so that your estate will not go to the people to whom you want it to go. It is therefore advisable to make a new will after divorce.

Even if you do not already have a will, it is advisable to make one after divorce for all the reasons why it is always advisable to make a will (appointing guardians for minor children, ensuring your estate is left to the people to whom you want it to go, tax planning, and so on).

RETAINING PAPERS

Copies of all documents relating to the divorce should ideally be kept. If this is not practical then you *must* retain the decree absolute and copies of any court orders, certainly until both parties remarry and preferably for life. It is possible to obtain an official copy of the decree absolute at any time after the divorce (for a small fee), but copies of orders can be harder or impossible to obtain many years after the divorce.

If, years after the divorce, you have mislaid your decree absolute and you can't recall when it was made or which court it was made in, then you may request a search of the central index of decrees absolute kept at the Principal Registry in London. For a search of any specified period of ten calendar years (or, if no such period is specified, for the ten most recent years) the fee is currently £40 including, if found, providing a certified copy of the decree absolute.

Appendix 1

Example Documents

1 EXAMPLE SEPARATION AGREEMENT

THIS DEED OF SEPARATION is made the   day of 2009

BETWEEN [name] of [address] (hereinafter called 'the husband') of the one part and also [name] of [address] (hereinafter called 'the wife') of the other part.

WHEREAS differences have arisen between the husband and the wife as a result of which they have agreed to live separate and apart from each other from the   day of

AND WHEREAS the husband and the wife have agreed that the provision referred to hereafter is accepted by them in full and final settlement of all claims of a financial nature by either party against the other.

NOW THIS DEED WITNESSETH AND IT IS HEREBY MUTUALLY AGREED as follows:

1.   That the husband and the wife shall hereafter be entitled to live separate and apart from one another as if they were unmarried.

2.   That neither the husband nor the wife shall molest, annoy or interfere with the other.

3.   That the children of the family [name] (date of birth) [name] (date of birth) shall reside with the wife who shall afford the husband reasonable contact with them.

4.   That the wife shall transfer to the husband within 28 days of the date of this deed all her legal estate and beneficial

interest in the freehold property at [address] subject to the mortgage secured thereon in favour of the Building Society and the husband shall pay or cause to be paid to the wife immediately following such transfer a lump sum of £100,000.

5.   That the contents of the said former matrimonial home shall be divided between the parties by agreement.

6.   That as from the date of separation referred to above the husband shall pay or cause to be paid periodical payments to the wife for the benefit of each of the said children until they shall attain the age of 18 years or cease full-time secondary education, whichever shall be the later, at the rate of £100 per month payable monthly.

7.   That on the 1st January of each year ('the variation date') the periodical payments set out in paragraph 7 above will stand varied automatically. The change in the payments shall be the change, if any, between the Retail Prices Index for 15 months before the date of the variation and the Retail Prices Index for the month three months before the variation date.

8.   That as from the date of separation referred to above the husband do pay or cause to be paid to the wife periodical payments at the rate of 5p per annum during their joint lives until the wife shall remarry or until the youngest child shall reach the age of 18 years whereupon the wife's claims for periodical payments and secured periodical payments shall stand dismissed and the wife shall not be entitled to make any further application under the Matrimonial Causes Act 1973 section 23(1)(a) or (b) in relation to the marriage

and the wife shall not be entitled to apply for an extension of the term of the said maintenance.

9.   That after two years have expired from the date of the separation referred to above either party to the marriage shall be at liberty to present the petition for divorce under the provisions of section 1(2)(d) of the Matrimonial Causes Act 1973 (as amended) and that the other party shall consent to a divorce on that basis and that each party will bear their own costs of their part in the said divorce decree proceedings save that each party will bear one half of the court fees.

10. That the husband and the wife will invite the court in such proceedings to dismiss all and any claims they may have against each other for financial provision and property adjustment.

IN WITNESS whereof the parties hereto have set their hands the day and year first before written.

SIGNED as a deed by the   )
husband in the presence of:)

SIGNED as a deed by the   )
wife in the presence of:)

2 EXAMPLE CONFESSION STATEMENT

I, Michael Henchard of 10 Dorchester Road, Casterbridge, Wessex, make this statement of my own free will, having been advised that it will be used in divorce proceedings.

I was married to Susan Henchard on the 29th day of February 1987.

Since about August 2008 I have committed adultery with a woman whose name and identity I do not wish to disclose.

Dated this 20th day of January 2009.

M. Henchard

3 EXAMPLE DIVORCE PETITION

In the Casterbridge County Court

~~In the Principal Registry~~   No. CA09D001

This petition is issued by Susan Henchard
('the petitioner')

The other party to the marriage is Michael Henchard
('the respondent')

(1)   On the 29th day of February 1987 Susan Henchard was
      lawfully married to Michael Henchard at the Register
      Office in the District of Casterbridge in the County of
      Wessex.

(1a) Since the date of the marriage the name of the petitioner
      has not changed.

(1b) The petitioner believes that since the date of the marriage
      the name of the respondent has not changed.

(2)   The petitioner and respondent last lived together as
      husband and wife at 25 Dorset Road, Casterbridge, Wessex.

(3)   The court has jurisdiction under Article 3(1) of the Council
      Regulation on the following grounds:

(4)   The petitioner and the respondent are both habitually
      resident in England and Wales.
      The petitioner is by occupation a learning support assistant
      and resides at 25 Dorset Road, Casterbridge, Wessex.
      The respondent is by occupation a bank manager and
      resides at 10 Dorchester Road, Casterbridge, Wessex.

(5)   There are no children of the family now living *except*
      James Henchard, who is over the age of 18 years;
      Lucy Henchard who was born on the 7th May 1991; and
      Lilly Henchard who was born on the 30th April 1998.

(6)   No other child, now living, has been born to the petitioner
      during the marriage.

(7)   There are or have been no other proceedings in any court
      in England and Wales or elsewhere with reference to the
      marriage (or to any child of the family) or between the
      petitioner and respondent with reference to any property
      of either or both of them.

(8)   There are or have been no proceedings in the Child
      Support Agency with reference to the maintenance of any
      child of the family.

(9)   There are no proceedings continuing in any country
      outside England and Wales which are in respect of
      the marriage or are capable of affecting its validity or
      substance.

(10) (Five years' separation cases only) ~~No agreement or~~
      ~~arrangement has been made or is proposed to be made~~
      ~~between the parties for the support of the Petitioner/~~
      ~~Respondent (and any child of the family)~~

(11) The said marriage has broken down irretrievably.

(12) The respondent has behaved in such a way that the
      petitioner cannot reasonably be expected to live with the
      respondent.

(13) Particulars

    (a)   Throughout the marriage the respondent has regularly drunk to excess. When drunk, the respondent has been violent and abusive towards the petitioner.

    (b)   One evening whilst the parties were on holiday in August 2008 the respondent became drunk at a restaurant. The petitioner asked him to return to the hotel but the respondent refused and shouted abuse at the petitioner, much to her embarrassment. When the parties did eventually return to the hotel an argument occurred between them, during the course of which the respondent held the petitioner against a wall and threatened her with his fist.

    (c)   Over the last 12 months the respondent has spent large sums of money on gambling, with the result that the family has suffered considerable financial hardship.

    (d)   Another argument occurred between the parties at Christmas 2008. The respondent was again drunk. During the argument the respondent grabbed the petitioner around the neck and threatened to kill her. After this incident, the petitioner asked the respondent to leave the matrimonial home, which he did, on the 1st January 2009. The parties have not lived together since that date.

PRAYER

The petitioner therefore prays:

(1) The suit

That the said marriage may be dissolved.

(2) Costs

That the respondent may be ordered to pay the costs of this suit.

(3) Ancillary relief

That the petitioner may be granted the following ancillary relief:

(a) an order for maintenance pending suit

a periodical payments order

a secured provision order

a lump sum order

a property adjustment order in respect of the property at 25 Dorset Road, Casterbridge, Wessex

an order under Section 24B, 25B or 25C of the Act of 1973 (pension sharing/ attachment order)

} for herself

(b) a periodical payments order

a secured provision order

a lump sum order

a property adjustment order

} for the children of the family

Signed   S.Henchard

The names and addresses of the persons to be served with the petition are:

Respondent: Michael Henchard, 10 Dorchester Road, Casterbridge, Wessex CA3 1WX.

Co-respondent:

The petitioner's address for service is: 25 Dorset Road, Casterbridge, Wessex CA2 2WX.

Dated this 1st day of February 2009.

Address all communications for the court to: The Court Manager, Casterbridge County Court, Prison Street, Casterbridge, Wessex CA1 1WX

[Backsheet]

In the Casterbridge County Court

No.

Between:

Susan Henchard

Petitioner

and

Michael Henchard

Respondent

DIVORCE PETITION

Full name and address of the petitioner:

Susan Henchard
25 Dorset Road
Casterbridge
Wessex
CA2 2WX

4 STATEMENT OF ARRANGEMENTS FOR CHILDREN

Statement of Arrangements for Children

In the	County Court
Petitioner	
Respondent	

No. of matter *(always quote this)*	

To the Petitioner

You must complete this form

If you or the respondent have any children
- under 16; or
- over 16 but under 18 if they are at school or college or are training for a trade, profession or vocation.

Please use black ink.

Please complete Parts I, II and III.
Before you issue a petition for divorce or dissolution try to reach agreement with your spouse/civil partner over the proposals for the children's future. There is space for him/her to sign at the end of this form if agreement is reached.
If your spouse/civil partner does not agree with the proposals he/she will have an opportunity at a later stage to state why he/she does not agree and will be able to make his/her own proposals.

You should take or send the completed form, signed by you (and, if agreement is reached, by your spouse/civil partner) together with a copy to the court when you issue your petition.
Please refer to the explanatory notes issued regarding completion of the prayer of the petition if you are asking the court to make any order regarding the children.

The Court will only make an order if it considers that an order will be better for the child(ren) than no order.
If you wish to apply for any of the orders which may be available to you under Part I or II of the Children Act 1989 you are advised to see a solicitor.
You should obtain legal advice from a solicitor or, alternatively, from an advice agency. Addresses of solicitors and advice agencies can be obtained from the Yellow Pages and the Solicitors Regional Directory which can be found at Citizens Advice Bureaux, Law Centres and any local library.

To the Respondent

The petitioner has completed Part I, II and III of this form, which will be sent to the Court at the same time that the petition for divorce or dissolution is filed.

Please read all parts of the form carefully.
If you agree with the arrangements and proposals for the children you should sign Part IV of the form.
Please use black ink. You should return the form to the petitioner, or his/her solicitor.
If you do not agree with all or some of the arrangements of proposals you will be given the opportunity of saying so when the petition for divorce or dissolution is served on you.

Part 1 - Details of the children
Please read the instructions for boxes 1, 2 and 3 before you complete this section

1.	**Children of both parties** *(Give details only of any children born to you and the Respondent or adopted by you both)*		
	Forenames	Surname	Date of birth
	(i)		
	(ii)		
	(iii)		
	(iv)		
	(v)		

2.	**Other children of the family** *(Give details of any other children treated by both of you as children of the family: for example your own or the Respondent's)*			
	Forenames	Surname	Date of birth	Relationship to Yourself Respondent
	(i)			
	(ii)			
	(iii)			
	(iv)			
	(v)			

3.	**Other children who are not children of the family** *(Give details of any children born to you or the Respondent that have not been treated as children of the family or adopted by you both)*		
	Forenames	Surname	Date of birth
	(i)		
	(ii)		
	(iii)		
	(iv)		
	(v)		

Part II - Arrangements for the children of the family

This part of the form must be completed. Give details for each child if arrangements are different.

(If necessary, continue on another sheet and attach it to this form.)

4.	Home details *(please tick the appropriate boxes)*	
	(a) The addresses at which the children now live	
	(b) Give details of the number of living rooms, bedrooms, etc. at the addresses in (a)	
	(c) Is the house rented or owned and by whom?	
	Is the rent or any mortgage being regularly paid?	☐ No ☐ Yes
	(d) Give the names of all other persons living with the children including your spouse/civil partner if he/she lives there. State their relationship to the children.	
	(e) Will there be any change in these arrangements?	☐ No ☐ Yes *(please give details)*

5.	**Education and training details** *(please tick the appropriate boxes)*
(a) Give the names of the school, college or place of training attended by each child.	
(b) Do the children have any special educational needs?	☐ No ☐ Yes *(please give details)*
(c) Is the school, college or place of training, fee-paying?	☐ No ☐ Yes *(please give details of how much the fees are per term/year)*
Are fees being regularly paid?	☐ No ☐ Yes *(please give details)*
(d) Will there be any change in these arrangements?	☐ No ☐ Yes *(please give details)*

6.	Childcare details *(please tick the appropriate boxes)*	
	(a) Which parent looks after the children from day to day? If responsibility is shared, please give details	
	(b) Does that parent go out to work?	□ No □ Yes *(please give details of his/her hours of work)*
	(c) Does someone look after the children when the parent is not there?	□ No □ Yes *(please give details)*
	(d) Who looks after the children during school holidays?	
	(e) Will there be any change in these arrangements?	□ No □ Yes *(please give details)*

7.	Maintenance *(please tick the appropriate boxes)*	
	(a) Does your spouse/civil partner pay towards the upkeep of the children? If there is another source of maintenance, please specify.	□ No □ Yes *(please give details of how much)*
	(b) Is the payment made under a court order?	□ No □ Yes *(please give details, including the name of the court and the case number)*
	(c) Is the payment following an assessment by the Child Support Agency?	□ No □ Yes *(please give details of how much)*
	(d) Has maintenance for the children been agreed?	□ No □ Yes
	(e) If not, will you be applying for: • a child maintenance order from the court	□ No □ Yes *(please give details)*
	• child support maintenance through the Child Support Agency?	□ No □ Yes *(please give details)*

8.	**Details for contact with the children** *(please tick the appropriate boxes)*	
	(a) Do the children see your spouse/civil partner?	□ No □ Yes *(please give details of how often and where)*
	(b) Do the children ever stay with your spouse/civil partner?	□ No □ Yes *(please give details of how much)*
	(c) Will there be any change to these arrangements? Please give details of the proposed arrangements for contact and residence.	□ No □ Yes *(please give details)*

9.	**Details of health** *(please tick the appropriate boxes)*

(a) Are the children generally in good health?	☐ No ☐ Yes *(please give details of any serious disability or chronic illness)*
(b) Do the children have any special health needs?	☐ No ☐ Yes *(please give details of the care needed and how it is to be provided)*

10.	**Details of care and other court proceedings** *(please tick the appropriate boxes)*

(a) Are the children in the care of a local authority, or under the supervision of a social worker or probation officer?	☐ No ☐ Yes *(please give details, including any court proceedings)*
(b) Are any of the children on the Child Protection Register?	☐ No ☐ Yes *(please give details of the local authority and the date of registration)*
(c) Are there or have there been any proceedings in any court involving the children, for example adoption, custody/ residence, access/contact, wardship, care, supervision or maintenance? (You need not include any Child Support Agency proceedings here)	☐ No ☐ Yes *(please give details and send a copy of any order to the Court)*

Part III To the Petitioner

Conciliation
If you and your spouse/civil partner do not agree   □ No   □ Yes
about arrangements for the child(ren), would you agree to
discuss the matter with a Conciliator and your
spouse/civil partner?

Declaration
I declare that the information I have given is correct and complete to the best
of my knowledge.

Signed (Petitioner)

Date:

Part IV To the Respondent

I agree with the arrangements and proposals contained in Part I and II of this
form.

Signed (Respondent)

Date:

5 AFFIDAVIT IN SUPPORT OF APPLICATION FOR DEEMED SERVICE

Affidavit of the petitioner

No: 1

Date Sworn:

Date Filed:

IN THE CASTERBRIDGE COUNTY COURT

Case No: CA09D001

BETWEEN:

Susan Henchard

Petitioner

and

Michael Henchard

Respondent

AFFIDAVIT OF THE PETITIONER IN SUPPORT OF

HER APPLICATION FOR DEEMED SERVICE

I SUSAN HENCHARD of 25 Dorset Road, Casterbridge, Wessex, the above named petitioner, MAKE OATH and SAY as follows:-

1. I filed my divorce petition with this court on the 1st February 2009. The court issued the petition on the 2nd February 2009 and a copy of the petition was posted to the respondent by the court on the 2nd February 2009. To date, the respondent has failed to file his acknowledgement of service with the court.

2. On the 4th February I received a telephone call from the respondent. He told me that he had received the divorce papers and that he had torn them up and thrown them in the bin.

3. In the circumstances, I would submit that the respondent has been served with the divorce papers and I would therefore ask this honourable court to direct that the petition shall be deemed to have been duly served upon the respondent, pursuant to Rule 2.9(6) Family Proceedings Rules 1991.

SWORN by the above named   )
SUSAN HENCHARD   )
At   )
In the County of   )
This   day of   2009)

Before me,

A Solicitor/Commissioner of Oaths.

6 EXAMPLE ACKNOWLEDGEMENT OF SERVICE

In the Casterbridge County Court

No. of matter:

Between:

Susan Henchard

Petitioner

and

Michael Henchard

Respondent

- If you intend to instruct a solicitor to act for you, give this form to him/her immediately.
- Read carefully the notice of proceedings before answering the following questions.
- Please complete using black ink.

1. Have you received the petition for divorce delivered with this form?	

1A. Are there any proceedings continuing in any country outside England and Wales which relate to the marriage or are capable of affecting its validity or subsistence? If so, please provide the following information:
  (a) particulars of the proceedings, including the court in or tribunal or authority before which they were begun,
  (b) the date when they were begun,
  (c) the names of the parties,
  (d) the date or expected date of any trial in the proceedings, and
  (e) such other facts as may be relevant to the question whether the proceedings on the petition should be stayed under Article 19 of the Council Regulation.	

1B. In which country are you –
  (a) habitually resident?
  (b) domiciled?
Of which country are you a national?	

1C. Do you agree with the statement of the petitioner as to the grounds of jurisdiction set out in the petition? If not, please state the grounds on which you disagree with the statement of the petitioner.	
2. On which date and at what address did you receive the petition?	
3. Are you the person named as the respondent in the petition?	
4. Do you intend to defend the case?	
5. (In the case of a petition alleging adultery) Do you admit the adultery alleged in the petition?	
6. Even if you do not intend to defend the case do you object to paying the costs of the proceedings? If so, on what grounds?	
7. (a) Have you received a copy of the statement of arrangements for the child(ren)?	
(b) What was the date of the statement of arrangements? (the date beside the petitioner's signature at Part 3)	
(c) Do you agree with the proposals in that statement of arrangements? **Notes** If **NO** you may file a written statement of your views on the present and the proposed arrangements for the children. It would help if you sent that statement to the court office with this form. You can get a form from the court office.	
8. (In the case of proceedings relating to a polygamous marriage) If you have any wife/husband in addition to the petitioner who is not mentioned in the petition, what is the name and address of each wife/husband and the date and place of your marriage to her/him?	

9(a) **You must complete this part if**
- you answered **Yes** to **Question 5**

or

- you answered **Yes** to **Question 7(c)**

or

- you do **not** have a solicitor acting for you

Signed: Date:

Address for service:*

*Note: If you are acting on your own you should also put your
                      place of residence, or if you do not reside in England
                      or Wales the address of a place in England or Wales to
                      which documents may be sent. If you subsequently
                      wish to change your address for service, you must
                      notify the Court.

9(b) I am/We are acting for the respondent in this matter.

Signed: Solicitor for the respondent

Date:
Address for service:

Note: If your client answered **Yes** to **Question 5** or **Question 7(c)** your client
must sign and date at **9(a)**.

Address all communications to the Court Manager **and quote the
case number**.

The Court Office at Prison Street, Casterbridge, Wessex CA1 1WX
is open from 10.00 am to 4.00 pm on Mondays to Fridays only.

Telephone:

7 APPLICATION FOR DIRECTIONS FOR TRIAL

No. of matter

IN THE	COUNTY COURT

Between ....……… Petitioner

and ....……… Respondent

Application for Directions for Trial (Special Procedure)

The petitioner   applies
to the District Judge for directions for the trial of this undefended
cause by entering it in the special procedure list.

The petitioner's affidavit of evidence is lodged with this
application.

Signed...Petitioner

Dated

If you write to the Court please address your letters to 'The Court
Manager' and quote the **No. of Matter** at the top of this form.

The Court Office is at Prison Street, Casterbridge, Wessex CA1
1WX and is open from 10.00 am to 4.00 pm on Monday to Friday.

8 AFFIDAVIT IN SUPPORT OF ADULTERY PETITION

In the County Court
[Principal Registry of the Family Division]

No. of Matter

Between

(Petitioner)

and

(Respondent)

and

(Co-Respondent)

Question	Answer
About the Divorce Petition 1. Have you read the petition in this case?	
2. Do you wish to alter or add to any statement in the petition? If so, state the alterations or additions.	

Question	Answer
3. Subject to these alterations or additions (if any) is everything stated **in your petition** true? If any statement is not within your own knowledge, indicate this and say whether it is true to the best of your information and belief.	
4. State briefly your reasons for saying that the respondent has committed the adultery alleged.	
5. On what date did it first become known to you that the respondent had committed the adultery alleged?	
6. Do you find it intolerable to live with the respondent?	
7. Since the date given in the answer to Question 5, have you ever lived with the respondent in the same household? If so, state the address and the period (or periods), giving dates.	

Question	Answer
About the children of the family 8. Have you read the statement of arrangements filed in this case?	
9. Do you wish to alter anything in the statement of arrangements or add to it? If so, state the alterations or additions	
10. Subject to these alterations and additions (if any) is everything stated in the **statement of arrangements** true? If any statement is not within your own knowledge, indicate this and say whether it is true and correct to the best of your information and belief.	

I,

of

make oath and say as follows:-

1. I am the petitioner in this cause.

2. **The answers to questions 1 to 10 above are true.**

3. I identify the signature...
appearing on the copy acknowledgment of service now produced
to me and marked 'A' as the signature of my husband/wife, the
respondent in this cause.

4. I identify the signature...
appearing at the foot of the document now produced to me and
marked 'B' as the signature of the respondent.

5. I identify the signature...
appearing at part IV of the statement of arrangements dated ....
now produced to me and marked 'C' as the signature of the
respondent.

6.

7. I ask the court to grant a decree dissolving my marriage with the
respondent on the ground stated in my petition [and to order the
respondent/co-respondent to pay the costs of this suit].

Sworn at   )
)
in the County of   )
)
this day of   , 20   )

....

Before me, ...

A Commissioner for Oaths
Officer of the Court appointed by
the Judge to take Affidavits.

9 AFFIDAVIT IN SUPPORT OF BEHAVIOUR PETITION

In the County Court
[Principal Registry of the Family Division]

No. of Matter

Between

(Petitioner)

and

(Respondent)

Question	Answer
About the Divorce Petition 1. Have you read the petition in this case including what is said about the behaviour of the respondent?	
2. Do you wish to alter or add to any statement in the petition? If so, state the alterations or additions.	
3. Subject to these alterations or additions (if any) is everything stated **in your petition** true? If any statement is not within your own knowledge, indicate this and say whether it is true to the best of your information and belief.	
4. If you consider that the respondent's behaviour has affected your health, state the affect that it has had.	

Question	Answer
5. (i) Is the respondent's behaviour as set out in your petition and particulars continuing? (ii) If the respondent's behaviour **is not continuing**, what was the date of the final incident relied upon by you in your petition?	
6. (i) Since the date given in the answer to question 5 or, if no date is given in answer to that question, since the date of the petition have you lived at the same address as the respondent for a period of more than 6 months, or for periods which together amount to more than 6 months? (ii) If so, state the address and the period (or periods), giving dates to the best of your knowledge or belief, and describe the arrangements for sharing the accommodation, including: • whether you have shared a bedroom; • whether you have taken your meals together; • what arrangements you have made for cleaning the accommodation and for other domestic tasks; • what arrangements you have made for the payment of household bills and other expenses.	
About the children of the family 7. Have you read the statement of arrangements filed in this case?	
8. Do you wish to alter anything in the statement of arrangements or add to it? If so, state the alterations or additions	
9. Subject to these alterations and additions (if any) is everything stated in the **statement of arrangements** true? If any statement is not within your own knowledge, indicate this and say whether it is true and correct to the best of your information and belief.	

I,

of

make oath and say as follows:-

1. I am the petitioner in this cause.

2. **The answers to questions 1 to 9 above are true.**

3. I identify the signature...
appearing on the copy acknowledgment of service now produced to
me and marked 'A' as the signature of my husband/wife, the respondent
in this cause.

4. I exhibit marked 'B' a certificate/report of Dr

5. I identify the signature...
appearing at part IV of the statement of arrangements dated ....
now produced to me and marked 'C' as the signature of the
respondent.

6. I ask the court to grant a decree dissolving my marriage with the
respondent on the ground stated in my petition [and to order the
respondent/co-respondent to pay the costs of this suit].

Sworn at   )
)
in the County of   )
)
this day of   , 20   )

....

Before me, ...

A Commissioner for Oaths
Officer of the Court appointed by
the Judge to take Affidavits.

10 AFFIDAVIT IN SUPPORT OF SEPARATION PETITION

In the County Court
[Principal Registry of the Family Division]

No. of Matter

Between

(Petitioner)

and

(Respondent)

Question	Answer
About the Divorce Petition 1. Have you read the petition in this case?	
2. Do you wish to alter or add to any statement in the petition? If so, state the alterations or additions.	
3. Subject to these alterations or additions (if any) is everything stated **in your petition** true? If any statement is not within your own knowledge, indicate this and say whether it is true to the best of your information and belief.	
4. State the date on which you and the respondent separated.	
5. State briefly the reason or main reason for the separation.	
6. State the date when and the circumstances in which you came to the conclusion that the marriage was in fact at an end.	

7. State as far as you know the various addresses at which you and the respondent have respectively lived since the last date given in the answer to Question 4, and the periods of residence at each address:

Petitioner's Address			Respondent's Address
From		From	
To		To	

8. Since the date given in the answer to question 4, have you ever lived with the respondent in the same household?

If so, state the address and the period (or periods), giving dates.

About the children of the family

9. Have you read the statement of arrangements filed in this case?

10. Do you wish to alter anything in the statement of arrangements or add to it?

If so, state the alterations or additions.

11. Subject to these alterations and additions (if any) is everything stated in the **statement of arrangements** true?

If any statement is not within your own knowledge, indicate this and say whether it is true and correct to the best of your information and belief.

I,

of

make oath and say as follows:-

1. I am the petitioner in this cause.

2. **The answers to questions 1 to 11 above are true.**

3. I identify the signature...
appearing on the copy acknowledgment of service now produced to
me and marked 'A'
as the signature of my husband/wife, the respondent in this cause.

4. I identify the signature...
appearing at part IV of the statement of arrangements dated ....
now produced to me and marked 'B' as the signature of the respondent.

5.

6. I ask the court to grant a decree dissolving my marriage with the
respondent on the ground stated in my petition [and to order the
respondent/co-respondent to pay the costs of this suit].

Sworn at   )
)
in the County of   )
)
this day of   , 20   )

....
Before me, ...

A Commissioner for Oaths
Officer of the Court appointed by
the Judge to take Affidavits.

11 NOTICE OF APPLICATION FOR DECREE NISI TO BE MADE ABSOLUTE

In the   County Court
[Principal Registry of the Family Division]

No. of matter

Between ....……… Petitioner

And .... Respondent

And .... Co-Respondent

TAKE NOTICE that the petitioner [or respondent] applies for –

1. the decree nisi pronounced in his [her] favour on the day of 20 , to be made absolute.

2. ~~the conditional order made in his [her] favour on the day of 20 , to be made final~~.

Dated this day of   20   .

Signed..
Petitioner
[or Respondent]

[Paragraph 2 relates to dissolution of civil partnerships, rather than divorce, and should therefore be deleted.]

12 EXAMPLE ANSWER AND CROSS PETITION

IN THE COUNTY COURT   **Case No:**

B E T W E E N:

Petitioner

and

Respondent

and

Party Cited

ANSWER AND CROSS-PETITION

The respondent in **ANSWER** to the petition filed in this suit says that:-

1. Paragraphs 1 to 12 of the petition are admitted.

2. The respondent denies that he has behaved himself in such a way that the petitioner cannot reasonably be expected to live with the respondent and specifically denies the allegations of behaviour contained in paragraph 13 of the petition.

3. The said marriage has broken down irretrievably by reason of the matters set out hereinafter.

4. The petitioner has committed adultery with [name] (hereinafter called 'the party cited') and the respondent finds it intolerable to live with the petitioner.

5. Since about the   day of   at an address or addresses unknown to the respondent the petitioner has committed adultery with the party cited.

The respondent therefore prays:-

1. That the prayer of the petition may be rejected.

2. That the marriage may be dissolved.

3. That the petitioner and the party cited may be ordered to pay the costs of this suit.

4. That the respondent may be granted the following ancillary relief:-
    i.   a lump sum order;
    ii. a property adjustment order;
    iii. an order under Section 24B, 25B or 25C of the   Act of 1973 (pension sharing/attachment order).

Signed..

Respondent

The names and addresses of the persons who are to be served with this answer and cross-petition are:-

(Petitioner)

(Party cited)

The address for service of the respondent is

Dated this day of   20

13 EXAMPLE CHILDREN APPLICATION

C100

Application under the Children Act 1989 for a residence, contact or other section 8 order

To be completed by the court	
Name of court	
Date issued	
Case number	
Child(ren)'s name(s)	Child(ren)'s number(s)

Before completing this application please read the booklet **'CB1 – Making an application – Children and the Family Courts'**. You can get a copy of all the forms and leaflets from your local court or they can be found at www.hmcourts-service.gov.uk

Cafcass/CAFCASS CYMRU will carry out checks as it considers necessary.

Cafcass - Children and Family Court Advisory and Support Service (in England); CAFCASS CYMRU - Children and Family Court Advisory and Support Service Wales.

Summary of application

Some people need permission to apply - See Section C of the booklet CB1

Have you applied to the court for permission to make this application? ☐ Yes ☐ Permission not required

Your name (the applicant(s))

The respondent's name(s)
See Sections G and H of the booklet CB1.

Please list the name(s) of the child(ren) and the type(s) of order you are applying for, starting with the oldest. To understand which order to apply for read the booklet CB1 Section D.

Name of child(ren)	Date of birth	Order(s) applied for
	D D / M M / Y Y Y Y	
	D D / M M / Y Y Y Y	
	D D / M M / Y Y Y Y	
	D D / M M / Y Y Y Y	
	D D / M M / Y Y Y Y	
	D D / M M / Y Y Y Y	

1. About you (the applicant)

Your first name	
Middle name(s)	
Surname	
Previous surnames (if any)	

Date of birth   D D / M M / Y Y Y Y   Sex ☐ Male ☐ Female

Place of birth
(town/county/country)

**If you do not wish your address to be made known to the
respondent,** leave the address details blank and complete
Confidential Address Form C8.

Address

Postcode ☐☐☐☐ ☐☐☐☐

Home telephone number

Mobile telephone number

Have you lived at this address
for more than 5 years?   ☐ Yes   ☐ No

If No, please provide details of all previous addresses you have lived at
for the last 5 years.

2

Your solicitor's details ────────

Do you have a solicitor acting for you?   ☐ Yes   ☐ No

If Yes, please give the following details

Your solicitor's name

Name of firm

Address

Postcode ☐☐☐☐ ☐☐☐☐

Telephone number

Fax number

DX number

Solicitor's Reference

Applicant 2 (if applicable) ────────

Your first name

Middle name(s)

Surname

Previous surnames (if any)

Date of birth   D D / M M / Y Y Y Y   Sex ☐ Male ☐ Female

Place of birth (town/county/country)

If your address details and those of your solicitor are different from the first applicant please provide details of these on a separate sheet.

What is your relationship to the applicant listed above?

3

2. The child(ren)

Please give details of the child(ren) and the order(s) you are applying for.
If there are more than 4 children please continue on a separate sheet.

Child 1

Child's first name	
Middle name(s)	
Surname	
Sex	☐ Male ☐ Female

What is your relationship to the child?	Applicant 1	Applicant 2

Is the child known by the Local Authority children's services? ☐ Yes ☐ No ☐ Don't know

If Yes, what is the name of the:

Local Authority	
Social worker (If known)	

Is the child subject of a child protection plan? ☐ Yes ☐ No ☐ Don't know

Who are the child's parents?

Who does the child live with?

Please give the full names of any other adults living at the same address and their relationship to the child.

4

Child 2 _____

Child's first name

Middle name(s)

Surname

Sex   ☐ Male   ☐ Female

Applicant 1	Applicant 2

What is your relationship to the child?

Is the child known by the Local Authority children's services?

☐ Yes   ☐ No   ☐ Don't know

If Yes, what is the name of the:

Local Authority

Social worker (If known)

Is the child subject of a child protection plan?

☐ Yes   ☐ No   ☐ Don't know

Who are the child's parents?

Who does the child live with?

Please give the full names of any other adults living at the same address and their relationship to the child.

Child 3

Child's first name	
Middle name(s)	
Surname	
Sex	☐ Male ☐ Female

	Applicant 1	Applicant 2
What is your relationship to the child?		

Is the child known by the Local Authority children's services?	☐ Yes ☐ No ☐ Don't know

If Yes, what is the name of the:

Local Authority	
Social worker (If known)	

Is the child subject of a child protection plan?	☐ Yes ☐ No ☐ Don't know

Who are the child's parents?	

Who does the child live with?	

Please give the full names of any other adults living at the same address and their relationship to the child.

6

Child 4 _____

Child's first name	
Middle name(s)	
Surname	
Sex	☐ Male ☐ Female

	Applicant 1	Applicant 2
What is your relationship to the child?		

Is the child known by the Local Authority children's services?	☐ Yes ☐ No ☐ Don't know

If Yes, what is the name of the:

Local Authority	
Social worker (If known)	
Is the child subject of a child protection plan?	☐ Yes ☐ No ☐ Don't know
Who are the child's parents?	
Who does the child live with?	
Please give the full names of any other adults living at the same address and their relationship to the child.	

3. Why are you making this application?

Please give brief details about why you are making this application. You should include details of:

- any previous agreements (formal or informal), and how they have broken down
- your reasons for bringing this application to the court
- what you want the court to do.

Do not give a full statement, please provide a summary. You may be asked to provide a full statement later.

4. Agreements about residence and/or contact

Have you received a copy of the 'Parenting Plan: Putting your children first: A guide for separating parents', booklet?

☐ Yes   ☐ No

If No, you can get a copy free of charge from your local court or you can download a copy from the website www.tso.co.uk

Have you used family mediation to attempt to agree arrangements for your children?

☐ Yes   ☐ No

If you would like to find out more about mediation please ask at your local court or see the website www.familymediationhelpline.co.uk.

Please give brief details about:
- If you attended family mediation what was the outcome?
- If you did not use mediation please explain why?

8

5. Risk

Do you believe that the child(ren) named at Section 2 have suffered or are at risk of suffering any harm from any of the following:

- any form of domestic abuse
- violence within the household
- child abduction
- other conduct or behaviour

by any person who has had contact with the child?

☐ Yes   ☐ No   ☐ Other

If Yes, please complete form C1A (Supplemental information form).

If Other, please give details

6. Other court cases which concern the child(ren) listed at Section 2

Are you aware of any other court cases now, or at any time in the past, which concern any of the child(ren) at Section 2?

☐ Yes   If Yes, please **attach a copy of any relevant order** and give additional details below

☐ No   If No, please **go to Section 7**

Additional details

Name of child(ren)

Name of the court where proceedings heard

Case no.

Date/year (if known)

Name of Cafcass/CAFCASS CYMRU officer

Name and address of child's solicitor, if known

Postcode ☐☐☐☐ ☐☐☐☐

If the above details are different for each child please provide details on additional sheets.

Please tick if additional sheets are attached.   ☐

9

7. The respondents

Sections G and H of the the booklet **'CB1 - Making an application - Children and the Family Courts'** explain who a respondent is.

If there are more than 2 respondents please continue on a separate sheet.

Respondent 1 _____

Respondent's first name

Middle name(s)

Surname

Previous surnames (if known)

Date of birth D D / M M / Y Y Y Y   Sex ☐ Male ☐ Female

Place of birth
(town/county/country, if known)

Address

Postcode ☐☐☐☐ ☐☐☐☐

Have they lived at this address
for more than 5 years?   ☐ Yes   ☐ No   ☐ Don't know

If No, please provide all previous addresses for the
last 5 years below, if known.

Relationship to the child(ren)

Name of child	Relationship

10

Respondent 2 _____

Respondent's first name	
Middle name(s)	
Surname	
Previous surnames (if known)	

Date of birth [D D / M M / Y Y Y Y]   Sex ☐ Male ☐ Female

Place of birth
(town/county/country, if known)

Address

Postcode [ ][ ][ ][ ] [ ][ ][ ][ ]

Have they lived at this address
for more than 5 years?   ☐ Yes   ☐ No   ☐ Don't know

If No, please provide all previous addresses for the
last 5 years below, if known.

Relationship to the child(ren)

Name of child	Relationship

11

8. Others who should be given notice

There may be other people who should be notified of your application, for example, someone who cares for the child but is not a parent. Sections G and I of the the booklet **'CB1 - Making an application - Children and the Family Courts'** explain who others are.

Person 1

Person's first name

Surname

Date of birth   D D / M M / Y Y Y Y   Sex ☐ Male ☐ Female

Address

Postcode ☐☐☐☐ ☐☐☐☐

Relationship to the child(ren)

Name of child	Relationship

Person 2

Person's first name

Surname

Date of birth   D D / M M / Y Y Y Y   Sex ☐ Male ☐ Female

Address

Postcode ☐☐☐☐ ☐☐☐☐

Relationship to the child(ren)

Name of child	Relationship

12

9. Signature

Print full name

Signed

Applicant

Date   D D / M M / Y Y Y Y

10. Attending the court

Section N of the the booklet **'CB1 - Making an application - Children and the Family Courts'** provides information about attending court.

If you require an interpreter, you must tell the court now so that one can be arranged.

Do you or any of the parties need an interpreter at court?

☐ Yes   ☐ No

If Yes, please specify the language and dialect:

If attending the court, do you or any of the parties involved have a disability for which you require special assistance or special facilities?

☐ Yes   ☐ No

If Yes, please say what the needs are

Please say whether the court needs to make any special arrangements for you to attend court (e.g. providing you with a separate waiting room from the respondent or other security provisions).

Court staff may get in touch with you about the requirements

continued over the page ⇨

What to do now

☐ Check you have attached copies of any **relevant orders** (as per Section 6).

☐ Check you have **signed** the form Section 9.

☐ You must provide a **copy** of the application and attached documents for each of the respondents and one for the Children and Family Court Advisory and Support Service (Cafcass or CAFCASS CYMRU).

☐ Is Form C1A attached (if applicable)?

☐ Details of the additional children if there are more than 4 in Section 2

☐ Details of the additional respondents if there are more than 2 in Section 7

☐ Check you have attached the correct fee. The leaflet 'EX50 County court fees' provides information about court fees you will have to pay.

Now take or send your application with the correct fee and correct number of copies to the court.

Court fees

You may be exempt from paying all or part of the fee. The combined booklet and application form 'EX160A Court Fees - Do you have to pay them' gives more information. You can get a copy from the court or download a copy from our website at www.hmcourts-service.gov.uk

14 Example consent order

IN THE CASTERBRIDGE COUNTY COURT

Case No:_CA09D001

BETWEEN:

Susan Henchard

Petitioner

and

Michael Henchard

Respondent

CONSENT ORDER

UPON the petitioner and the respondent agreeing that the terms of this order are accepted in full and final satisfaction of all claims for income, capital and pension sharing orders and of any other nature whatsoever which either may be entitled to bring against the other or the other's estate arising in relation to their marriage.

AND UPON the petitioner and the respondent agreeing that the contents of the former matrimonial home known as 25 Dorset Road, Casterbridge, Wessex shall remain the absolute property of the party in whose possession they now are.

AND UPON the petitioner undertaking to the court and agreeing to use her best endeavours to procure the release of the respondent within 56 days from the date of decree absolute from any liability under the mortgage secured upon 25 Dorset Road, Casterbridge, Wessex in favour of Wessex Building Society and to indemnify the Respondent against all such liability.

BY CONSENT IT IS ORDERED subject to decree absolute that:

1. The petitioner do pay or cause to be paid to the respondent a lump sum of £10,000 within 56 days of the date of decree absolute.

2. The respondent do transfer to the petitioner upon payment of the lump sum referred to in paragraph 1 above all his legal estate and beneficial interest in the freehold property 25 Dorset Road, Casterbridge, Wessex registered at H.M. Land Registry under title number WX1234 subject to the mortgage secured thereon in favour of Wessex Building Society.

3. Upon payment of the lump sum and completion of the transfer of 25 Dorset Road, Casterbridge, Wessex as provided for by paragraphs 1 and 2 of this order and upon the making of a final decree herein the petitioner's and the respondent's claims for financial provision, pension sharing and property adjustment orders do stand dismissed and neither the petitioner nor the respondent shall be entitled to make any further application in relation to their marriage under the Matrimonial Causes Act 1973 s.23(1)(a) or (b) or to make an application to the court, on the death of the other, for provision out of his or her estate.

4. There be no order as to costs insofar as this application and the negotiations ancillary thereto are concerned.

Dated this 20th day of August 2009.

Signed.............................   Signed.............................

Petitioner   Respondent

15 STATEMENT OF INFORMATION FOR A CONSENT ORDER

In the [County Court]

[Principal Registry of the Family Division]
No. of matter

Between   Petitioner *Solicitor's ref*
and   Respondent *Solicitor's ref*

Statement of Information for a Consent Order
Duration of Marriage or Civil Partnership

In the case of a marriage: Give the date of your marriage and the date of the decree absolute (if pronounced).

In the case of a civil partnership: Give the date of the formation of the civil partnership and the date of the final order (if made).

		(1) Capital Resources *(less any unpaid mortgage or charge)*	(2) Net Income	(3) Pension
Ages of parties *Give the age of any minor (i.e. under the age of 18) or dependant child(ren) of the family.*	Petitioner Respondent Child(ren)			
Summary of means *Give, as at the date this statement is signed overleaf:* *(1) the approximate amount or value of **capital resources**. If there is a property give its net equity and details of the proposed distribution of the equity.*	Petitioner			
*(2) the **net income** of the petitioner and respondent and, where relevant, of minor or dependant child(ren) of the family.* *(3) the value of any benefits under a **pension arrangement** which you have, or are likely to have, including the most recent valuation (if any) provided by the pension scheme.*	Respondent			
***Note:** if the application is only made for an order for interim periodical payments, or for variation of an order for periodical payments, you only need to give details of 'net income'.*	Children			

Where the parties and the children will live
Give details of the arrangements which are intended for the accommodation of each of the parties and any minor or dependant child(ren) of the family.

Future plans *Please tick a box and, if appropriate, give the date of the marriage or formation of the civil partnership, if you know it.*	**No intention to marry, form a civil partnership, or cohabit at present**	**Has remarried or formed a civil partnership**	**Intends to marry or form a civil partnership**	**Intends to cohabit with another person**
Petitioner	☐	☐ Date of marriage or formation of civil partnership:	☐ Date of marriage or formation of civil partnership:	☐ Date of marriage or formation of civil partnership:
Respondent	☐	☐ Date of marriage or formation of civil partnership:	☐ Date of marriage or formation of civil partnership:	☐ Date of marriage or formation of civil partnership:

Notice to Mortgagee *These questions are to be answered by the applicant where the terms of the order provide for a transfer of property.*	Has every mortgagee (if any) of the property been served with notice of the application?	Yes ☐ No ☐
	Has any objection to a transfer of property been made by any mortgagee, within **14** days from the date when the notice of the application was served?	Yes ☐ No ☐

Notice to Pension Arrangement *These questions are to be answered by the applicant where the terms of an order include provision for a pension attachment order.*	Has every person responsible for any pension arrangement been served with notice of the application and notice under Rule 2.70(7)(a) to (d) of the Family Proceedings Rules 1991?	Yes ☐	No ☐
	Has any objection to an order under – (i) section 23 of the Matrimonial Causes Act 1973 which includes provision by virtue of section 25B and section 25C of that Act; or (ii) Part 1 of Schedule 5 to the Civil Partnership Act 2004 which includes provision by virtue of paragraphs 25 and 26 of Schedule 5 to that Act – (as the case may be) been made by a trustee or manager within **21** days from the date when the notice of the application was served?	Yes ☐	No ☐
Pension Sharing on Divorce or Dissolution *These questions are to be answered by the applicant where the terms of the order include provision for a pension sharing order.*	Has the pension arrangement furnished the information required by Regulation 4 of the Pensions on Divorce etc. (Provisions of Information) Regulations 2000?	Yes ☐	No ☐
	Does it appear from that information that there is power to make an order including provision under section 24B of the Matrimonial Causes Act 1973 or under paragraph 15 of Schedule 5 to the Civil Partnership Act 2004 (Pension Sharing)?	Yes ☐	No ☐

Other information
Give details of any other especially significant matters

Signed

[Solicitor for] Petitioner Date	[Solicitor for] Respondent Date

16 FORM A – APPLICATION FOR ANCILLARY RELIEF

Notice of [intention to proceed with] an Application for Ancillary Relief	In the *[County Court] *[Principal Registry of the Family Division]

Case No.	

Respondents (Solicitor(s)) name and address

Applicant's solicitor's reference	
Respondent's solicitor's reference	

Between (applicant)

and (respondent)

Take Notice that the applicant intends:

*to apply to the Court for

*to proceed with the application in the [petition][answer] for

*to apply to vary:

delete as appropriate

☐ an order for maintenance pending suit or outcome of proceedings

☐ a periodical payments order

☐ a secured provision order

☑ a lump sum order

☐ a property adjustment order *(please provide address)*

☐ a pension sharing order or a pension attachment order

If an application is made for any periodical payments or secured periodical payments for children:

• and there is a written agreement made before 5 April 1993 about maintenance for the benefit of children, **tick this box** ☐

• and there is a written agreement made on or after 5 April 1993 about maintenance for the benefit of children, **tick this box** ☐

• but there is no agreement, tick any of the boxes below to show if you are applying for payment:

☐ for a stepchild or stepchildren

☐ in addition to child support maintenance already paid under a Child Support Agency assessment

☐ to meet expenses arising from a child's disability

☐ to meet expenses incurred by a child in being educated or training for work

☐ when either the child **or** the person with care of the child **or** the absent parent of the child

☐ is not habitually resident in the United Kingdom

☐ Other *(please state)*

Signed:

Dated:

[Applicant/Solicitor for the Applicant]

17 Form E – Financial statement

Financial Statement

OF

In the
*[High/County Court]
*[Principal Registry of the Family Division]

Case No. *Always quote this*	
Petitioner's solicitor's reference	
Respondent's solicitor's reference	

*Husband/*Wife

*(*delete as appropriate)*

Between

	and	

Who is the *husband/*wife/*civil partner*petitioner/*respondent in the*divorce/*dissolution suit Applicant in this matter

Who is the *husband/*wife/*civil partner*petitioner/*respondent in the*divorce/*dissolution suit Respondent in this matter

Please fill in this form fully and accurately. Where any box is not applicable, write 'N/A'.

You have a duty to the court to give a full, frank and clear disclosure of all your financial and other relevant circumstances.

A failure to give full and accurate disclosure may result in any order the court makes being set aside.

If you are found to have been deliberately untruthful, criminal proceedings for perjury may be taken against you.

You must attach documents to the form where they are specifically sought and you may attach other documents where it is necessary to explain or clarify any of the information that you give.

Essential documents that must accompany this statement are detailed in the form.

If there is not enough room on the form for any particular piece of information, you may continue on an attached sheet of paper.

If you are in doubt about how to complete any part of this form you should seek legal advice.

This statement must be sworn before a solicitor, a commissioner for oaths or an officer of the court or, if abroad, a notary or duly authorised official, before it is filed with the court or sent to the other party (see last page).

This statement is filed by

Name and address of solicitor

1 General Information

1.1 Full name

1.2 Date of birth

Date	Month	Year

1.3 Date of the marriage

Date	Month	Year

1.4 Occupation

1.5 Date of the separation

Date	Month	Year

Tick here if not applicable ☐

1.6 Date of the

Petition			Decree nisi/Decree of judicial separation Conditional order/ Separation order			Decree absolute/ Final order (if applicable)		
Date	Month	Year	Date	Month	Year	Date	Month	Year

1.7 If you have subsequently married or formed a civil partnership, or will do so, state the date

Date	Month	Year

1.8 Are you co-habiting? Yes ☐ No ☐

1.9 Do you intend to co-habit within the next six months? Yes ☐ No ☐

1.10 Details of any children of the family

Full names	Date of birth			With whom does the child live?
	Date	Month	Year	

1.11 Details of the state of health of yourself and the children if you think this should be taken into account

Yourself	Children

1.12 Details of the present and proposed future educational arrangements for the children.

Present arrangements	Future arrangements

1.13 Details of any child support maintenance calculation or any maintenance order or agreement made in respect of any children of the family. If no calculation, order or agreement has been made, give an estimate of the liability of the non-resident parent in respect of the children of the family under the Child Support Act 1991.

1.14 If this application is to vary an order, attach a copy of the order and give details of the part that is to be varied and the changes sought. You may need to continue on a separate sheet.

1.15 Details of any other court cases between you and your spouse/civil partner, whether in relation to money, property, children or anything else.

Case No	Court

1.16 Your present residence and the occupants of it and on what terms you occupy it.

Address	Occupants	Terms of occupation

2 Financial Details *Part 1 Real Property and Personal Assets*

2.1 Complete this section in respect of the family home (the last family home occupied by you and your spouse/civil partner) if it remains unsold.

Documentation required for attachment to this section:
- a) A copy of any valuation of the property obtained within the last six months. If you cannot provide this document, please give your own realistic estimate of the current market value
- b) A recent mortgage statement confirming the sum outstanding on each mortgage

Property name and address	
Land Registry title number	
Mortgage company name(s) and address(es) and account number(s)	
Type of mortgage	
Details of who owns the property and the extent of your legal and beneficial interest in it (i.e. state if it is owned by you solely or jointly owned with your spouse/ civil partner or with others) If you consider that the legal ownership as recorded at the Land Registry does not reflect the true position, state why	
Current market value of the property	
Balance outstanding on any mortgage(s)	
If a sale at this stage would result in penalties payable under the mortgage, state amount	
Estimate the costs of sale of the property	
Total equity in the property (i.e. market value less outstanding mortgage(s), penalties if any and the costs of sale)	
TOTAL value of your interest in the family home: Total A	£

2.2 Details of your interest in any other property, land or buildings. Complete one page for each property you have an interest in.

Documentation required for attachment to this section:
(a) A copy of any valuation of the property obtained within the last six months. If you cannot provide this document, please give your own realistic estimate of the current market value
(b) A recent mortgage statement confirming the sum outstanding on each mortgage

Property name and address	
Land Registry title number	
Mortgage company name(s) and address(es) and account number(s)	
Type of mortgage	
Details of who owns the property and the extent of your legal and beneficial interest in it (i.e. state if it is owned by you solely or jointly owned with your spouse/civil partner or with others)	
If you consider that the legal ownership as recorded at the Land Registry does not reflect the true position, state why	
Current market value of the property	
Balance outstanding on any mortgage(s)	
If a sale at this stage would result in penalties payable under the mortgage, state amount	
Estimate the costs of sale of the property	
Total equity in the property (i.e. market value less outstanding mortgage(s), penalties if any and the costs of sale)	
Total value of your interest in this property	

TOTAL value of your interest in ALL other property:
Total B   £

2.3 Details of all personal bank, building society and National Savings Accounts that you hold or have held at any time in the last twelve months and which are or were either in your own name or in which you have or have had any interest. This applies whether any such account is in credit or in debit. For joint accounts give your interest and the name of the other account holder. If the account is overdrawn, show a minus figure.

Documentation required for attachment to this section:
For each account listed, all statements covering the last 12 months.

Name of bank or building society, including branch name	Type of account (e.g. current)	Account number	Name of other account holder (if applicable)	Balance at the date of this statement	Total current value of your interest

				TOTAL value of your interest in ALL accounts:	£

2.4 Details of all investments, including shares, PEPs, ISAs, TESSAs, National Savings Investments (other than already shown above), bonds, stocks, unit trusts, investment trusts, gilts and other quoted securities that you hold or have an interest in. (Do not include dividend income as this will be dealt with separately later on.)

Documentation required for attachment to this section:
Latest statement or dividend counterfoil relating to each investment.

Name	Type of investment	Size of holding	Current value	Name of any other account holder (if applicable)	Total current value of your interest
				TOTAL value of your interest in ALL holdings: (C2)	£

2.5   **Details of all life insurance policies including endowment policies that you hold or have an interest in. Include those that do not have a surrender value. Complete one page for each policy.**

Documentation required for attachment to this section:

A surrender valuation of each policy that has a surrender value.

Name of company	
Policy type	
Policy number	
If policy is assigned, state in whose favour and amount of charge	
Name of any other owner and the extent of your interest in the policy	

Maturity date *(if applicable)*	Date	Month	Year

Current surrender value *(if applicable)*	
If policy includes life insurance, the amount of the insurance and the name of the person whose life is insured	
Total current surrender value of your interest in this policy	
TOTAL value of your interest in ALL policies: (C3)	£

2.6 **2.6 Details of all monies that are OWED TO YOU. Do not include sums owed in director's or partnership accounts which should be included at section 2.11.**

Brief description of money owed and by whom	Balance outstanding	Total current value of your interest

TOTAL value of your interest in ALL debts owed to you: (C4)	£

2.7 **Details of all cash sums held in excess of £500. You must state where it is held and the currency it is held in.**

Where held	Amount	Currency	Total current value of your interest

TOTAL value of your interest in ALL cash sums: (C5) £

2.8 Details of personal belongings individually worth more than £500.

INCLUDE:
• Cars (gross value)
• Collections, pictures and jewellery
• Furniture and house contents

Brief description of item	Total current value of your interest
TOTAL value of your interest in ALL personal belongings: (C6)	£
Add together all the figures in boxes C1 to C6 to give the TOTAL current value of your interest in personal assets: TOTAL C	£

2 Financial Details *Part 2 Capital: Liabilities and Capital Gains Tax*

2.9 Details of any liabilities you have.

EXCLUDE liabilities already shown such as:
• **Mortgages**
• **Any overdrawn bank, building society or National Savings accounts**

INCLUDE:
• **Money owed on credit cards and store cards**
• **Bank loans**
• **Hire purchase agreements**

List all credit and store cards held including those with a nil or positive balance. Where the liability is not solely your own, give the name(s) of the other account holder(s) and the amount of your share of the liability.

Liability	Name(s) of other account holder(s) *(if applicable)*	Total liability	Total current value of your interest in the liability
TOTAL value of your interest in ALL liabilities: (D1)			£

2.10 If any Capital Gains Tax would be payable on the disposal now of any of your real property or personal assets, give your estimate of the tax liability.

Asset	Total Capital Gains Tax liability
TOTAL value of ALL your potential Capital Gains Tax liabilities: (D2)	£
Add together D1 and D2 to give the TOTAL value of your liabilities: TOTAL D	£

2 Financial Details *Part 3 Capital: Business assets and directorships*

2.11 Details of all your business interests. Complete one page for each business you have an interest in.

Documentation required for attachment to this section:
- a)   Copies of the business accounts for the last two financial years
- b)   b) Any documentation, if available at this stage, upon which you have based your estimate of the current value of your interest in this business, for example a letter from an accountant or a formal valuation. It is not essential to obtain a formal valuation at this stage

Name of the business	
Briefly describe the nature of the business	
Are you *(Please delete all those that are not applicable)*	a) Sole trader b) Partner in a partnership with others c) Shareholder in a limited company
If you are a partner or a shareholder, state the extent of your interest in the business (i.e. partnership share or the extent of your shareholding compared to the overall shares issued)	
State when your next set of accounts will be available	
If any of the figures in the last accounts are not an accurate reflection of the current position, state why. For example, if there has been a material change since the last accounts, or if the valuations of the assets are not a true reflection of their value (e.g. because property or other assets have not been re-valued in recent years or because they are shown at a book value)	
Total amount of any sums owed to you by the business by way of a director's loan account, partnership capital or current accounts or the like. Identify where these appear in the business accounts	
Your estimate of the current value of your business interest. Explain briefly the basis upon which you have reached that figure	
Your estimate of any Capital Gains Tax that would be payable if you were to dispose of your business now	
Net value of your interest in this business after any Capital Gains Tax liability	

TOTAL value of ALL your interests in business assets: TOTAL E	£

2.12 List any directorships you hold or have held in the last 12 months (other than those already disclosed in Section 2.11).

2 Financial Details *Part 4 Capital: Pensions*

2.13 Give details of all your pension rights. Complete a separate page for each pension.

EXCLUDE:
• Basic State Pension
INCLUDE (complete a separate page for each one):
• Additional State Pension (SERPS and State Second Pension (S2P))
• Free Standing Additional Voluntary Contribution Schemes (FSAVC) separate from the scheme of your employer
• Membership of ALL pension plans or schemes

Documentation required for attachment to this section:
a)   A recent statement showing the cash equivalent transfer value (CETV) provided by the trustees or managers of each pension arrangement (or, in the case of the additional state pension, a valuation of these rights)
b)   b) If any valuation is not available, give the estimated date when it will be available and attach a copy of your letter to the pension company or administrators from whom the information was sought and/or state the date on which an application for a valuation of a State Earnings Related Pension Scheme was submitted to the Department of Work and Pensions

Name and address of pension arrangement	
Your National Insurance Number	
Number of pension arrangement or reference number	
Type of scheme e.g. occupational or personal, final salary, money purchase, additional state pension or other (if other, please give details)	
Date the CETV was calculated	
Is the pension in payment or drawdown or deferment? *(Please answer Yes or No)*	
State the cash equivalent transfer value (CETV) quotation, or in the additional state pension, the valuation of those rights **If the arrangement is an occupational pension arrangement that is paying reduced CETVs, please quote what the CETV would have been if not reduced. If this is not possible, please indicate if the CETV quoted is a reduced CETV**	

TOTAL value of ALL your pension assets: TOTAL F | £ |

2 Financial Details *Part 5 Capital: Other assets*

2.14 Give details of any other assets not listed in Parts 1 to 4 above.

INCLUDE (the following list is not exhaustive):
• Any personal or business assets not yet disclosed
• Unrealisable assets
• Share option schemes, stating the estimated net sale proceeds of the shares if the options were capable of exercise now, and whether Capital Gains Tax or income tax would be payable
• Business expansion schemes
• Futures
• Commodities
• Trust interests (including interests under a discretionary trust), stating your estimate of the value of the interest and when it is likely to become realisable. If you say it will never be realisable, or has no value, give your reasons
• Any asset that is likely to be received in the foreseeable future
• Any asset held on your behalf by a third party
• Any asset not disclosed elsewhere on this form even if held outside England and Wales

You are reminded of your obligation to disclose all your financial assets and interests of ANY nature.

Type of asset	Value	Total NET value of your interest
TOTAL value of ALL your other assets: TOTAL G		£

2 Financial Details *Part 6 Income: Earned income from employment*

2.15 Details of earned income from employment. Complete one page for each employment.

Documentation required for attachment to this section:
- a)   P60 for the last financial year (you should have received this from your employer shortly after the last 5th April)
- b)   b) Your last three payslips
- c)   c) Your last Form P11D if you have been issued with one

Name and address of your employer	
Job title and brief details of the type of work you do	
Hours worked per week in this employment	
How long have you been with this employer?	
Explain the basis of your income i.e. state whether it is based on an annual salary or an hourly rate of pay and whether it includes commissions or bonuses	
Gross income for the last financial year as shown on your P60	
Net income for the last financial year i.e. gross income less income tax and national insurance	
Average net income for the last three months i.e. total income less income tax and national insurance divided by three	
Briefly explain any other entries on the attached payslips other than basic income, income tax and national insurance	
If the payslips attached for the last three months are not an accurate reflection of your normal income briefly explain why	
Details and value of any bonuses or other occasional payments that you receive from this employment not otherwise already shown, including the basis upon which they are paid	
Details and value of any benefits in kind, perks or other remuneration received from this employer in the last year (e.g. provision of a car, payment of travel, accommodation, meal expenses, etc.)	
Your estimate of your net income from this employment for the next 12 months. If this differs significantly from your current income explain why in box 4.1.2	

Estimated TOTAL of ALL net earned income from employment for the next 12 months: TOTAL H   £

2 Financial Details *Part 7 Income: Income from self-employment or partnership*

2.16 You will have already given details of your business and provided the last two years accounts at section 2.11. Complete this section giving details of your income from your business. Complete one page for each business.

Documentation required for attachment to this section:

a) A copy of your last tax assessment or, if that is not available, a letter from your accountant confirming your tax liability

b) If net income from the last financial year and estimated net income for the next 1months is significantly different, a copy of management accounts for the period since your last account

Name of the business	
Date to which your last accounts were completed	
Your share of gross business profit from the last completed accounts	
Income tax and national insurance payable on your share of gross business profit above	
Net income for that year (using the two figures directly above, gross business profit less income tax and national insurance payable)	
Details and value of any benefits in kind, perks or other remuneration received from this business in the last year e.g. provision of a car, payment of travel, accommodation, meal expenses, etc.	
Amount of any regular monthly or other drawings that you take from this business	
If the estimated figure directly below is different from the net income as at the end date of the last completed accounts, briefly explain the reason(s)	
Your estimate of your net annual income for the next 12 months	

Estimated TOTAL of ALL net income from self-employment or partnership for the next 12 months: TOTAL I | £

2 Financial Details *Part 8 Income: Income from investments e.g. dividends, interest or rental income*

2.17 Details of income received in the last financial year (the year ended last 5th April), and your estimate of your income for the current financial year. Indicate whether the income was paid gross or net of income tax. You are not required to calculate any tax payable that may arise.

Nature of income and the asset from which it derived	Paid gross or net	Income received in the last financial year	Estimated income for the next 12months
Estimated TOTAL investment income for the next 12 months: TOTAL J			£

2 Financial Details *Part 9 Income: Income from state benefits (including state pension and child benefit)*

2.18 Details of all state benefits that you are currently receiving.

Name of benefit	Amount paid	Frequency of payment	Estimated income for the next 12months
Estimated TOTAL benefit income for the next 12 months: TOTAL K			£

2 Financial Details *Part 10 Income: Any other income*

2.19 Details of any other income not disclosed above.

INCLUDE:
• Any source from which income has been received during the last 12 months (even if it has now ceased)
• Any source from which income is likely to be received during the next 12 months

You are reminded of your obligation to give full disclosure of your financial circumstances.

Nature of income	Paid gross or net	Income received in the last financial year	Estimated income for the next 12months
Estimated TOTAL other income for the next 12 months: **TOTAL L**			£

2 Financial Details *Summaries*

2.20 Summary of your capital (Parts 1 to 5)

Description	Reference of the section on this statement	Value
Current value of your interest in the family home	A	
Current value of your interest in all other property	B	
Current value of your interest in personal assets	C	
Current value of your liabilities	D	
Current value of your interest in business assets	E	
Current value of your pension assets	F	
Current value of all your other assets	G	
TOTAL value of your assets (Totals A to G less D):		£

2.21 Summary of your estimated Income for the next 12 months (Parts 6 to 10)

Description	Reference of the section on this statement	Value
Estimated net total of income from employment	H	
Estimated net total of income from self-employment or partnership	I	
Estimated net total of investment income	J	
Estimated state benefit receipts	K	
Estimated net total of all other income	L	
Estimated TOTAL income for the next 12 months (Totals H to L):		£

3 Financial Requirements *Part 1 Income needs*

3.1 Income needs for yourself and for any children living with you or provided for by you. ALL figures should be annual, monthly or weekly (state which). You *must not* use a combination of these periods. State your current income needs and, if these are likely to change in the near future, explain the anticipated change and give an estimate of the future cost.

The income needs below are: Weekly   Monthly   Annual *(delete those not applicable)*
I anticipate my income needs are going to change because

3.1.1 Income needs for yourself.
INCLUDE:
• All income needs for yourself
• Income needs for any children living with you or provided for by you only if these form part of your total income needs (e.g. housing, fuel, car expenses, holidays, etc)

Item	Current cost	Estimated future cost
SUB-TOTAL your income needs:	£	

3.1.2 Income needs for children living with you or provided for by you.
INCLUDE:
• Only those income needs that are different to those of your
household shown above

Item	Current cost	Estimated future cost
SUB-TOTAL children's income needs:	£	
TOTAL of ALL income needs:	£	

3 Financial Requirements *Part 2 Capital needs*

3.2 Set out below the reasonable future capital needs for yourself and for any children living with you or provided for by you.

3.2.1 Capital needs for yourself.
INCLUDE:
• All capital needs for yourself
• Capital needs for any children living with you or provided for by you only if these form part of your total capital needs (e.g. housing, car etc.)

Item	Cost
SUB-TOTAL your capital needs:	£

3.2.2 Capital needs for children living with you or provided for by you.

INCLUDE:
• Only those capital needs that are different to those of your household shown above

Item	Cost
SUB-TOTAL your children's capital needs:	£
TOTAL of ALL capital needs:	£

4 Other Information

4.1 Details of any significant changes in your assets or income.

At both sections 4.1.1 and 4.1.2, INCLUDE:
• ALL assets held both within and outside England and Wales
• The disposal of any asset

4.1.1 Significant changes in assets or income during the LAST 12 months.

4.1.2 Significant changes in assets or income likely to occur during the NEXT 12 months.

4.2 Brief details of the standard of living enjoyed by you and your spouse/civil partner during the marriage/civil partnership.

4.3 Are there any particular contributions to the family property and assets or outgoings, or to family life, or the welfare of the family that have been made by you, your partner or anyone else that you think should be taken into account? If there are any such items, briefly describe the contribution and state the amount, when it was made and by whom.
INCLUDE:
• Contributions already made
• Contributions that will be made in the foreseeable future.

4.4 Bad behaviour or conduct by the other party will only be taken into account in very exceptional circumstances when deciding how assets should be shared after divorce/dissolution. If you feel it should be taken into account in your case, identify the nature of the behaviour or conduct below.

4.5 Give details of any other circumstances that you consider could significantly affect the extent of the financial provision to be made by or for you or any child of the family.
INCLUDE (the following list is not exhaustive):
• Earning capacity
• Disability
• Inheritance prospects
• Redundancy
• Retirement
• Any plans to marry, form a civil partnership or cohabit
• Any contingent liabilities.

4.6 If you have subsequently married or formed a civil partnership (or intend to) or are living with another person (or intend to), give brief details, so far as they are known to you, of his or her income, assets and liabilities.

Annual Income		Assets and Liabilities	
Nature of income	Value (if known, state whether gross or net)	Item	Value (if known)
Total income:	£	**Total assets/ liabilities:**	£

5 Order Sought

5.1 If you are able at this stage, specify what kind of orders you are asking the court to make.

Even if you cannot be specific at this stage, if you are able to do so, indicate:
- a) If the family home is still owned, whether you are asking for it to be transferred to yourself or your spouse/civil partner or whether you are saying it should be sold
- b) Whether you consider this is a case for continuing spousal maintenance/ maintenance for your civil partner or whether you see the case as being appropriate for a 'clean break'. *(A 'clean break' means a settlement or order which provides amongst other things, that neither you nor your spouse/civil partner will have any further claim against the income or capital of the other party. A 'clean break' does not terminate the responsibility of a parent to a child.)*
- c) Whether you are seeking a pension sharing or pension attachment order
- d) If you are seeking a transfer or settlement of any property or assets, identify the property or assets in question.

5.2 If you are seeking a variation of an ante-nuptial or post-nuptial settlement or a relevant settlement made during, or in anticipation of, a civil partnership, identify the settlement, by whom it was made, its trustees and beneficiaries and state why you allege it is a settlement which the court can vary.

5.3 If you are seeking an avoidance of disposition order, or if you have already applied for such an order, identify the property to which the disposition relates and the person or body in whose favour the disposition is alleged to have been made.

Sworn confirmation of the information

I [   ] *(the above-named applicant/ respondent)*

of [   ] MAKE OATH and confirm that the information given above is a full, frank, clear and accurate disclosure of my financial and other relevant circumstances.

Sworn by the above named

at   )
)
)
)
)
this   day of   20   )

Before me, ...

A solicitor, commissioner for oaths, an Officer of the Court appointed by the Judge to take affidavits, a notary or duly authorised official.

Address all communications to the Court Manager of the Court and quote the case number.
If you do not quote this number, your correspondence may be returned.

Schedule of Documents to accompany Form E

The following list shows the documents you must attach to your Form E if applicable. You may attach other documents where it is necessary to explain or clarify any of the information that you give in the Form E.

Form E paragraph	Document	Please tick		
		Attached	Not applicable	To follow
1.14	**Application to vary an order:** if applicable, attach a copy of the relevant order.			
2.1	**Matrimonial home valuation:** a copy of any valuation relating to the matrimonial home that has been obtained in the last six months.			
2.1	**Matrimonial home mortgage(s):** a recent mortgage statement in respect of each mortgage on the matrimonial home confirming the amount outstanding.			
2.2	**Any other property:** a copy of any valuation relating to each other property disclosed that has been obtained in the last six months.			
2.2	**Any other property:** a recent mortgage statement in respect of each mortgage on each other property disclosed confirming the amount outstanding.			
2.3	**Personal bank, building society and National Savings accounts:** copies of statements for the last 12 months for each account that has been held in the last 12 months, either in your own name or in which you have or have had any Interest.			
2.4	**Other investments:** the latest statement or dividend counterfoil relating to each investment as disclosed in paragraph 2.4.			
2.5	**Life insurance (including endowment) policies:** a surrender valuation for each policy that has a surrender value as disclosed under paragraph 2.5.			
2.11	**Business interests:** a copy of the business accounts for the last two financial years for each business interest disclosed.			
2.11	**Business interests:** any documentation that is available to confirm the estimate of the current value of the business, for example, a letter from an accountant or formal valuation if that has been obtained.			

2.13	**Pension rights:** a recent statement showing the cash equivalent transfer value (CETV) provided by the trustees or managers of each pension arrangement that you have disclosed (or, in the case of the additional state pension, a valuation of these rights). If not yet available, attach a copy of the letter sent to the pension company or administrators requesting the information.			
2.15	**Employment income:** your P60 for the last financial year in respect of each employment that you have.			
2.15	**Employment income:** your last three payslips in respect of each employment that you have.			
2.15	**Employment income:** your last form P11D if you have been issued with one.			
2.16	**Self-employment or partnership income:** a copy of your last tax assessment or if that is not available, a letter from your accountant confirming your tax liability.			
2.16	**Self-employment or partnership income:** if net income from the last financial year and the estimated income for the next twelve months is significantly different, a copy of the management accounts for the period since your last accounts.			
State relevant Form E paragraph	**Description of other documents attached:**			

Case no.

In the

*[High/County Court]
*[Principal Registry of the Family Division]

In the marriage/Civil Partnership between

who is the husband/wife/civil partner
and

who is the husband/wife/civil partner

Financial Statement on behalf of

who is the husband/wife/civil partner
and the petitioner/respondent in
the divorce/dissolution suit

This statement is filed by

18 EXAMPLE CHRONOLOGY

IN THE CASTERBRIDGE COUNTY COURT

Case No:_CA09D001

BETWEEN:

Susan Henchard

Applicant

and

Michael Henchard

Respondent

APPLICANT'S CHRONOLOGY

----

1. The parties were married on the 29th day of February 1987.

2. There are three children of the family, namely James Henchard, who is over the age of 18 years and independent, Lucy Henchard who was born on the 7th May 1991 and Lilly Henchard who was born on the 30th April 1998.

3. The parties separated on the 1st January 2009, when the respondent left the former matrimonial home. The respondent is now living in rented accommodation. The applicant remains in the former matrimonial home.

4. The applicant filed her divorce petition on the basis of unreasonable behaviour, on the 1st day of February 2009.

5. The decree nisi was pronounced on the 1st May 2009.

6. The applicant issued her application for ancillary relief on the 5th May 2009.

7. The First Appointment has been fixed for the 4th August 2009.

Dated this   2009.

…………………………………..

Applicant

19 EXAMPLE STATEMENT OF ISSUES

IN THE CASTERBRIDGE COUNTY COURT

Case No: CA09D001

BETWEEN:

Susan Henchard

Applicant

and

Michael Henchard

Respondent

APPLICANT'S CONCISE STATEMENT OF ISSUES

----

1. Whether or not there should be a clean break.

2. Whether or not the applicant should receive a lump sum payment from the respondent.

3. In respect of the former matrimonial home, the applicant claims that the property is worth £250,000 and the respondent claims that it is worth £300,000.

4. The applicant disputes the respondent's claimed income, as disclosed by the respondent in his Form E.

5. Whether or not the respondent is cohabiting with another person.

6. Whether or not there should be a pension sharing order in the applicant's favour in respect of the respondent's pension.

Dated this 8th day of July 2009.

....

Applicant

20 EXAMPLE QUESTIONNAIRE

IN THE CASTERBRIDGE COUNTY COURT

Case No: CA09D001

BETWEEN:

Susan Henchard

Applicant

and

Michael Henchard

Respondent

_____

APPLICANT'S QUESTIONNAIRE

_____

1. With regard to section 1.8 of the respondent's Form E, please confirm that he is, in fact, cohabiting with his new partner 'Wendy'. If so, please provide details of the respondent's partner's means, as required by section 4.6 of the respondent's Form E.

2. With regard to section 2.3 of the respondent's Form E:

    (i) Please explain the following withdrawals from his bank account:-
        (a) £1500.00 on the 15th December 2008;
        (b) £5,000.00 on the 31st January 2009.

    (ii) Please confirm that the respondent has no other bank accounts and explain what happened to his Casterbridge Bank Plc Savings account – if this account is still open, please provide 12 months' statements and if it is closed, please provide a copy of the closing statement.

3. With regard to section 2.13 of the respondent's Form E, please provide documentary evidence of the cash equivalent transfer value of the respondent's pension, from his pension provider.

4. With regard to section 2.15 of the respondent's Form E:
    (i)   Please provide copies of his last three payslips.
    (ii) Please also explain how the respondent arrives at his estimated net income figure for next year.
    (iii) Please explain why the respondent's income dropped when the divorce proceedings commenced.

5. With regard to section 3.1.1 of the respondent's Form E, please explain the following:
    (i)   Why his telephone expenses are so high; and
    (ii) Why his petrol expenses are so high, particularly having regard to the fact that he receives a mileage allowance; and
    (iii) Why his food/housekeeping bill is so high for one person, and how the respondent arrived at this figure; and
    (iv) How the respondent can afford to pay outgoings totalling £2,000 per month from an income of only £20,000 per annum.

Dated this 8th day of October 2009

....
Applicant

21 FORM G – NOTICE OF RESPONSE TO FIRST APPOINTMENT

<table>
<tr><td rowspan="4">**Notice of response to First Appointment**</td><td colspan="2">In the

*[County Court]
*[Principal Registry of the Family Division]</td></tr>
<tr><td>Case No.</td><td></td></tr>
<tr><td>Applicant's solicitor's reference</td><td></td></tr>
<tr><td>Respondent's solicitor's reference</td><td></td></tr>
</table>

The marriage of   **and**

Take Notice that

At the First Appointment which will be heard on   20

at   [am][pm]

the [applicant] [respondent] [will] [will not] be in a position to proceed on that occasion with a Financial Dispute Resolution appointment for the following reasons:

Dated:

Useful Addresses and Websites

Cafcass (Children and Family Court Advisory and Support Service)

Details:	Looks after the interests of children involved in family proceedings.
Address:	Cafcass National Office 8th Floor South Quay Plaza 3 189 Marsh Wall London E14 9SH
Telephone:	020 7510 7000
Website:	www.cafcass.gov.uk

Child Maintenance and Enforcement Commission

Details:	Established to take over responsibility for the child maintenance system, from the Child Support Agency.
Address:	Currently can only be contacted via website
Website:	www.childmaintenance.org
Email:	Via website

Child Maintenance Options

Details: Provides impartial information and support
                 to help both parents make informed choices about
                 child maintenance.
Address: Contact via phone or website
Telephone: 0800 988 0988
Website: www.cmoptions.org
Email: Via website

Child Support Agency

Details: Calculates and collects child maintenance.
Address: National Helpline
                 PO Box 55
                 Brierly Hill DY5 1YL
Telephone: 08457 133 133 (General enquiries)
Website: www.csa.gov.uk
Email: Via website

Citizens Advice Bureaux

Details: Provides independent advice on your rights. To
                 find your local Citizens Advice Bureau, search the
                 Directory on their website.
Website: www.citizensadvice.org.uk/index/getadvice

Community Legal Advice

Details: A free and confidential service paid for by legal
                 aid. Website includes a calculator to calculate
                 whether you are eligible for legal aid and a
                 directory of legal aid suppliers.
Telephone: 0845 345 4 345
Website: www.communitylegaladvice.org.uk

Courts Service

Details: Includes court addresses and telephone numbers,
                forms, guides and details of fees.

Website: www.hmcourts-service.gov.uk

Families Need Fathers

Details: Fathers' rights group. Site includes advice,
                support and other resources.

Address: 134 Curtain Road
                London EC2A 3AR

Telephone: 020 7613 5060

Helpline: 08707 607496

Website: www.fnf.org.uk

Email: fnf@fnf.org.uk

Family Lore

Details: My blog! Includes advice and reference pages.

Website: www.familylore.co.uk

Family Mediation Helpline

Details: Information on mediation, and 'find a mediator'
                service.

Telephone: 0845 60 26 627

Website: www.familymediationhelpline.co.uk

E-mail: info@familymediationhelpline.co.uk

The Law Society

Details: Represents solicitors in England and Wales.
                Website includes 'find a solicitor' section.

Address: The Law Society's Hall
                113 Chancery Lane
                London WC2A 1PL
Telephone: 020 7422 1222
Website: www.lawsociety.org.uk

One Parent Families | Gingerbread

Details: Charity working to help lone parents and their
                children.
Address: 255 Kentish Town Road
                London NW5 2LX
Telephone: 020 7428 5400
Helpline: 0800 018 5026
Website: www.oneparentfamilies.org.uk
Email: info@oneparentfamilies.org.uk

Relate

Details: UK's largest provider of relationship counselling
                and sex therapy. Also offers a range of other
                relationship support services.
Telephone: Central Office: 0300 100 1234
Website: www.relate.org.uk

Resolution

Details: Association of family lawyers committed to the
                constructive resolution of family disputes.
Address: Central Office
                PO Box 302
                Orpington
                Kent BR6 8QX

Telephone: 01689 820272
Website: www.resolution.org.uk

Email: info@resolution.org.uk

Women's Aid

Details: National charity working to end domestic
               violence against women and children.
Telephone: 0808 2000 247 (Free phone 24 hr National
               Domestic Violence Helpline)
Website: www.womensaid.org.uk

Appendix 3

Glossary

Adultery – Defined as 'consensual sexual intercourse between a married person and a person of the opposite sex, not being the other's spouse'. Note that it is still adultery even if the husband and wife are living separately. One of the five ways of proving that the marriage has irretrievably broken down, for the purpose of divorce proceedings.

Affidavit – A document to which the writer swears (usually on a Bible) that the contents are true. Note that making a false statement in an affidavit amounts to perjury.

Ancillary relief – The financial/property settlement in connection with divorce proceedings.

Answer – A document that must be filed with the court by a respondent who is defending divorce proceedings, setting out their response to the allegations contained in the petition. See also Cross Petition.

Applicant – The party issuing an application to the court, such as an application for a contact order or an application for ancillary relief. Note that the party issuing the divorce itself is called the 'petitioner', but if they then issue an application for ancillary relief, they will be the applicant in the ancillary relief proceedings. If the other party issues an application for ancillary relief, they will be the respondent in the ancillary relief proceedings, which can be confusing!

Attachment of earnings – Method of enforcement of (usually) maintenance orders or child support, whereby the debtor's employer is required to deduct a regular sum of money from the debtor's earnings.

Backsheet – The last page of a court document, giving details of the court, the case number, the parties' names, the title of the document and the full name and address of the person filing the document. The backsheet always faces outwards, so that it can be read without opening the document.

Cafcass (The Children and Family Court Advisory and Support Service) – Looks after the interests of children involved in family proceedings.

Cash equivalent transfer value (CETV) – A means of valuing a pension, required by the court in any ancillary relief proceedings. Strictly, it is the amount that could be transferred out of that pension fund into another.

Charging order – Method of enforcement of a debt. The creditor takes a charge over property owned by the debtor, for the amount of the debt. The creditor can then apply for an order that the property be sold, so that the debt is repaid.

Child support – Also known as child maintenance, child support is a regular payment to the parent with whom the child(ren) is/

are living (the parent with care (PWC)) from the other parent (the non-resident parent (NRP)).

Clean break – A financial/property settlement that dismisses all claims for maintenance by either spouse against the other, thus achieving a 'clean break' between the parties.

Conciliation – Similar to mediation. The term most often refers to an in-court process whereby the judge and/or a Cafcass officer discusses the issues informally with the parents and, if appropriate, tries to help them reach agreement.

Consent order – A court order made with the agreement of both parties. Note that the order must still be approved by the court, which is not obliged to approve it merely because the parties agree.

Contact activity – A direction requiring an individual who is a party to the proceedings to take part in an activity that promotes contact with the child concerned, for example, attending relevant parenting programmes or classes, or information sessions, before a contact order is made.

Contact order – An order requiring the person with whom a child lives, or is to live, to allow the child to visit or to stay with the person named in the order, or to allow such other contact between the child and that person (for example, telephone contact) as the court specifies. Essentially the same as what used to be known as 'access'.

Co-respondent – The person named by the petitioner as having committed adultery with the respondent. The co-respondent is a party to the divorce proceedings.

Cross petition – A document filed by a respondent who wishes to defend the divorce and cross-petition, alleging that the breakdown of the marriage was due to a different reason to that alleged by the petitioner in the petition. Usually combined with an answer (see above entry).

Decree absolute – The order finalising the divorce.

Decree nisi – The order stating that the petitioner (or the respondent, in the case of a divorce proceeding on a cross petition) is entitled to the divorce.

Deduction from earnings order – Method of enforcing payment of child support by deducting money from the non-resident parent's earnings.

Desertion – Essentially, separation without consent or good reason, and where the deserting spouse has no intention of returning.

Directions – Orders of the court, usually setting out how the case will proceed.

Domestic violence – Defined as: 'Any incident of threatening behaviour, violence or abuse (psychological, physical, sexual, financial or emotional) between adults who are or have been intimate partners or family members, regardless of gender or sexuality.'

Domicile – The country in which you live, or would be living if you were not (temporarily) living where you are currently – i.e. the country to which you intend to return, having not emigrated on a permanent basis.

Enforcement order – An order enabling the court, upon application, to impose an unpaid work requirement on a person who breaches a contact order.

Exhibit – A document attached to an affidavit, normally marked with a letter and referred to as such in the affidavit.

Family law protocol – Good practice guide for lawyers doing family law work.

Financial Dispute Resolution appointment – A hearing within an application for ancillary relief, at which the parties should use their best endeavours to settle the matter by agreement, with the help of the court.

Garnishee order – Method of enforcement whereby (most commonly) a sum of money is taken from the debtor's bank account, in settlement of the debt.

Habitual residence – The country in which you habitually (as opposed to temporarily) reside.

Injunction – An order requiring a party to do, or to refrain from doing, certain acts. In family law, most commonly refers to domestic violence orders (see non-molestation order and occupation order).

Irretrievable breakdown (of marriage) – The ground for divorce. Must be proved by proving adultery, unreasonable behaviour, two years' desertion, two years' separation with the other party's consent or five years' separation.

Jurisdiction – Before a court can deal with a matter, it must have jurisdiction, i.e. the power to deal with the matter. Particularly relevant in cases with an international element, when the party issuing the proceedings must prove that the English court has jurisdiction, rather than (or as well as) a foreign court.

Legal aid – State assistance with legal costs, usually only available to those on benefits and low income. Also known as 'public funding'.

Liability order – Order of a magistrates' court confirming that child support is owed, and enabling the Child Support Agency to take further enforcement action.

Lump sum order – An order requiring one party to pay to the other a lump sum of money, whether in one go or by instalments.

Matrimonial assets (or matrimonial property) – Assets of the marriage that fall to be divided between the parties on divorce, as opposed to assets that will remain the property of the owning party.

Mediation – A process whereby a trained mediator will help a divorcing or separating couple agree arrangements for children and/or a financial/property settlement.

Non-molestation order – A court order prohibiting one party from molesting, harassing or pestering the other party.

Non-resident parent (NRP) – The parent with whom the child or children is/are not residing. A term usually used in connection with child support (see above). Replaced the term 'absent parent'.

Occupation order – An order requiring a party to vacate or not to return to the matrimonial home. Also known as an 'ouster order'.

Offsetting – An arrangement whereby one party retains or receives a larger share of one asset, in return for the other party retaining another asset. Usually used in connection with pensions, whereby, for example, a wife may have a larger share of the former matrimonial home, in return for the husband retaining his pension.

Parental responsibility – Defined as 'all the rights, duties, powers, responsibilities and authority which by law a parent of a child has in relation to the child and his property'. Shared by both parents where they are married.

Parent with care (PWC) – The parent with whom the child or children is/are living. A term usually used in connection with child support (see above).

Party cited – A non-spouse who is made party to the divorce proceedings because the respondent alleges that they have committed adultery with the petitioner.

Pension attachment order – States that one party will receive part of the other party's pension when the other party receives it.

Pension sharing order – An order transferring all or part of one party's pension to the other party.

Periodical payments – Another term for maintenance.

Petitioner – The party who issues the divorce proceedings. The other party will be the 'respondent'.

Pre-application protocol – Obliges both parties to make a reasonable effort to reach a financial/property settlement by agreement before an application for ancillary relief is made.

Prohibited steps order – Defined as 'an order that no step which could be taken by a parent in meeting his parental responsibility for a child, and which is of a kind specified in the order, shall be taken by any person without the consent of the court'. A typical example is an order prohibiting a parent from taking any step that may result in the child being known by a new name.

Property adjustment order – An order adjusting the ownership of matrimonial property.

Residence order – An order that the child or children reside with a particular person or persons, usually one of the parents (or both, in the case of shared residence). Residence orders replaced, but are not quite the same as, custody orders.

Respondent – The party who did not issue the proceedings. Note that the respondent to an application for ancillary relief could also be the petitioner in the divorce proceedings.

Specific issue order – Defined as 'an order giving directions for the purpose of determining a specific question which has arisen, or which may arise, in connection with any aspect of parental responsibility for a child'. An example of such an issue is a dispute between the parents over their child's schooling – the court will decide which school the child should attend.

Supplemental petition – A document setting out further allegations which occurred after the date of the original petition.

Unreasonable behaviour – Behaviour by one party such that the other party cannot reasonably be expected to live with them. One of the five ways of proving that the marriage has irretrievably broken down, for the purpose of divorce proceedings.

Warrant of execution – Method of enforcement of a debt whereby a bailiff can seize property owned by the debtor, up to the value of the debt. The property is then sold, so that the debt can be repaid.

Without prejudice – Words used in an offer of settlement to ensure that the offer cannot be shown to the court if it is not accepted. If the offer is accepted the protection of 'without prejudice' is gone. Note that without prejudice proposals are not considered to be appropriate in proceedings relating to children.

List of Divorce County Courts

You can issue the divorce proceedings in any of these courts, but you may wish to use your nearest court, as you may need to attend the court. Details of the addresses of the courts can be found on the Courts Service website – see Appendix 2.

Aberystwyth County Court
Accrington County Court
Aldershot and Farnham County Court
Altrincham County Court

Barnet Civil and Family Courts Centre
Barnsley County Court
Barrow-in-Furness County Court
Bath County Court
Birkenhead County Court
Birmingham Family Courts
Bishop Auckland County Court
Blackburn County Court
Blackpool County Court
Blackwood Civil and Family Court
Bodmin County Court
Bournemouth County Court
Bradford Combined Court Centre
Brecon Law Courts
Brentford County Court

Bridgend Law Courts
Brighton County Court Family Centre
Bristol County Court
Bromley County Court
Burnley Combined Court Centre
Bury County Court
Bury St Edmunds County Court

Caernarfon County Court
Cambridge County Court
Canterbury Combined Court Centre
Cardiff Civil Justice Centre
Carlisle Combined Court Centre
Carmarthen County Court
Chelmsford County and Family Proceedings Court
Chester Civil Justice Centre
Clerkenwell and Shoreditch County Court
Consett County Court
Crewe County Court
Croydon County Court

Dartford County Court
Dewsbury County Court
Durham County Court

Epsom County Court

Gateshead County Court
Gloucestershire Family and Civil Courts
Great Grimsby Combined Court Centre
Guildford County Court

Harlow County Court
Hartlepool County Court
Haverfordwest County Court
Hitchin County Court

Kendal County Court

Lancaster County Court
Leicester County Court
Leigh County Court
Liverpool Civil and Family Court
Llanelli County Court
Llangefni County Court
Lowestoft County Court
Luton County Court

Maidstone Combined Court Centre
Manchester Civil Justice Centre
Medway County Court
Milton Keynes County Court
Morpeth and Berwick County Court

Neath and Port Talbot County Court
Newcastle-upon-Tyne Combined Court Centre
Newport (Gwent) County Court
Newport (Isle of Wight) Crown and County Court
North Shields County Court

Oxford Combined Court Centre

Penzance County Court
Plymouth Combined Court
Pontefract County Court
Pontypridd County Court
Portsmouth Combined Court Centre
Preston Combined Court Centre
Principal Registry of the Family Division, London

Rawtenstall County Court
Rhyl County Court
Rotherham County Court

Salford County Court
Salisbury Crown & County Court
Scarborough County Court
Scunthorpe County Court
Shrewsbury County Court
South Shields County Court
Southampton Combined Court Centre
Southend County Court
Southport County Court
St Helens County Court
Staines County Court
Stoke-on-Trent Combined Court
Sunderland County Court
Swansea Civil Justice Centre
Swindon Combined Court

Tameside County Court
Trowbridge County Court
Tunbridge Wells County Court

Uxbridge County Court

Wakefield County Court
Welshpool and Newtown County Court
Weymouth and Dorchester Combined Court Centre
Whitehaven County Court
Wigan County Court
Winchester Combined Court Centre
Wolverhampton Combined Court Centre
Worthing County Court
Wrexham County Court

Yeovil County Court
York County Court

Index